THE
BROKENHEARTED
EVANGELIST

THE
BROKENHEARTED
EVANGELIST

JEREMY WALKER

Reformation Heritage Books
Grand Rapids, Michigan

Reformation Heritage Books
2965 Leonard St. NE
Grand Rapids, MI 49525
616-977-0889 / Fax 616-285-3246
orders@heritagebooks.org
www.heritagebooks.org

Printed in the United States of America
14 15 16 17 18 19/10 9 8 7 6 5 4 3 2

Library of Congress Cataloging-in-Publication Data

Walker, Jeremy (Jeremy R.), 1975-
 The brokenhearted evangelist / Jeremy Walker.
     p. cm.
 Includes bibliographical references and index.
 ISBN 978-1-60178-161-1 (pbk. : alk. paper) 1. Evangelistic work. I. Title.
 BV3790.W317 2012
 269'.2—dc23
                           2011053435

For additional Reformed literature, request a free book list from Reformation Heritage Books at the above regular or e-mail address.

CONTENTS

PREFACE

Do you know and believe that there is nothing that glorifies God more than the accomplishment of His saving purposes in His Son, Jesus Christ? Do you know and believe that there is nothing more important to a person than the destiny of his immortal soul? Do you know and believe that there is a heaven to be gained and a hell from which to flee, and that our relationship to the Lord Jesus is the difference between the two? Do you know and believe that only those who repent of their sins and believe in the Lord Jesus Christ will be saved? Do you know and believe that God sends His saints into the world in order to preach that gospel by which sinners are saved?

It is easy to answer such questions with a gutless orthodoxy. Lively faith in Christ grasps spiritual realities in a way that galvanizes the believer. All truth—whether of God's grace to us or of our duty to God—bears fruit in us only insofar as we are connected to Christ by faith. This being so, says John Owen, "he alone understands divine truth who doeth it: John vii.17. There is not, therefore, any one text of Scripture which presseth our duty unto God, that we can so understand as to perform that duty in an acceptable manner, without an actual regard unto Christ, from whom alone we receive ability for the performance of it, and in or through whom alone it is accepted with God."[1]

We cannot pretend that we have understood divine truth unless we are living it. We cannot pretend that we know and believe the truth

---

1. John Owen, *Christologia: or, A Declaration of the Glorious Mystery of the Person of Christ—God and Man*, in *The Works of John Owen* (Edinburgh: Banner of Truth, 1965), 1:82.

about men, souls, heaven, hell, and salvation unless it is making a difference in the way we think, feel, pray, speak, and act.

A vigorous, practical concern for the lost, growing out of a desire
for God's glory in man's salvation, is an eminently Christlike thing and
a hallmark of healthy Christianity. By such a standard, there are many
unhealthy churches and unhealthy Christians; by such a standard, and
to my great grief, I am not well myself.

While I accept that there can be an unbalanced and crippling
expectation and even unbiblical obsession with some aspects of evangelism and "mission" (as the portentous modern singular would have it),
there is an opposite and perhaps greater danger in our day that believers
and churches enjoying possession of a great deposit of truth nevertheless do not *know* it. If they did, they would be doing something.

It is very easy to be up in arms, for example, about current assaults
on what can so calmly be described as the doctrine of hell. "Of course
there is a hell!" we protest, offended and disturbed that someone could
deny what is so plainly written in the Word of God. Is there a hell?
What difference has it made? What have we done differently because
there is a hell? Is its reality driving our thoughts, words, and deeds?
Many of us who have entered the kingdom have come perilously close
to the flames of the pit. We have felt its fire, and yet we have, perhaps,
forgotten that from which we have been delivered. The urgency with
which we fled to Christ ourselves has perhaps been replaced with a
casual awareness of spiritual reality that never energizes us to do anything for those who are themselves in danger of eternal punishment.

The same could be said of heaven, of Christ's atonement for sinners,
of God's grace and mercy, of the freeness of the gospel, of the excellence
of salvation. "Yes…yes…yes," the monotonous ticking off of doctrines
received continues. But what difference does it make to you and me?

It is my heartfelt contention that the truths we believe ought to
make the people of God brokenhearted evangelists. My prayer for this
book is that the Lord Christ would make its author and its readers truly
understand the gospel duty that God has laid upon His church and
therefore make us willing to perform the work we have been given to

do. By His strength may God make us able to do it, to the praise of the glory of His grace.

My thanks are due to Seth Getz, who strongly urged me to develop this material and encouraged me along the way; to the several friends who analyzed and assessed various portions and gave their feedback generously and robustly; to the believers, past and present, whom I have come to know remotely or immediately, who in their spirit and activity exemplify the truths I have labored to communicate; and to my wife, who patiently bears with and encourages a husband who fails more often than he succeeds to embrace all the aspects of the work he has been given to do.

———◆———

To those who go out in order to compel the needy to come in.

May God grant success to such labors, that His house may be full.

———◆———

CHAPTER 1

AM I WILLING?
Our Undeniable Obligation

His life hangs by a thread, but he sleeps. The fumes rising from the fire smoldering below are creeping into his lungs, slowing his heart and dulling his mind. The flames themselves are catching hold, sucking the oxygen from the air, building in ferocity and intensity, enveloping and devouring with insatiable appetite. Soon those fumes will capture him, and those flames will consume him. He desperately needs to be saved. What will you do? How will you communicate his need to be delivered?

If you were outside his home, watching the flickering blaze and billowing smoke of the fire, would you stand there, the picture of non-chalance, discussing his prospects for survival? Or would you do all that lay in your power to save the man? What would your words and actions communicate? Would their tone and vigor suggest carelessness, ease, and triviality, or would they indicate pressure and urgency—even desperation? What kind of person would stand casually and carelessly by while another was choked and consumed only a few feet away? Under such circumstances, any right-thinking, right-feeling person would be the model of earnest endeavor, laboring with all that was in him to rouse the sleeper, alert him to danger, obtain assistance, and provide help.

Felt Urgency Communicated

So it is with the brokenhearted evangelist. Scripture and church history provide examples of those who labored with a present and pressing sense of the choking reality of sin and the consuming fires of hell. We could never accuse them of nonchalance. They did not display a casual attitude. They grieved over every moment lost, every opportunity missed. They labored with the urgency of eternity near at hand, pressing upon their souls.

So we see the humbled and earnest Peter, restored to usefulness following his denials of Christ, charging the house of Israel with the awful reality that the very Jesus whom they crucified God had made both Lord and Christ, with the result that those who heard him were cut to the heart (Acts 2:36–37). We find the apostle Paul, a saved persecutor and blasphemer, a man redeemed from zealous but sterile self-righteousness, crying out with sorrow in his soul that he could wish himself accursed from Christ for the sake of his brother Israelites (Rom. 9:1–5). There he is, ready to become all things to all men that he might by all means save some (1 Cor. 9:22).

What brought from Richard Baxter's heart this earnest declaration: "I preached as never sure to preach again, and as a dying man to dying men"?[1] Or what of John Bunyan, author of *The Pilgrim's Progress*, who testified, "I preached what I felt, what I smartingly [acutely, deeply] did feel. Indeed, I have been to them as one sent to them from the dead; I went myself in chains to preach to them in chains, and carried that fire in my own conscience that I persuaded them to beware of"?[2]

Or, later, there is George Whitefield, as described by his friend John Gillies:

> The burning desire to reach the hosts of mankind with the message of saving grace overruled all trials that came in the way, and he testified to the Divine assistance he experienced in learning the task [of preaching in the open air without notes], and the joy that was his as he performed it, saying:… "Sometimes, when twenty thousand people were before me, I had not, in my own apprehension, a word to say either to God or them. But I was never totally deserted, and frequently…so assisted, that I knew by happy experience what our Lord meant by saying, 'Out of his belly shall flow rivers of living water.'… The sight of thousands and thousands, some in coaches, some on horseback, and some in the trees, and at

1. Richard Baxter, "Love Breathing Thanks and Praise," part 2, stanza 29.
2. John Bunyan, *Grace Abounding to the Chief of Sinners* (London: Penguin, 1987), 70.

times all affected and drenched in tears together, to which sometimes was added the solemnity of the approaching evening, was
almost too much for, and quite overcame me."[3]

These were men called by God to proclaim the good news of everlasting life through faith in Jesus Christ. They carried out that calling
with a profound and pressing sense of urgency, constrained by the
awareness that not a moment could be lost.

Such a spirit, however, is not restricted to a single vocation—the
preacher—or a single location—the pulpit. Remember the example of
Monica, the mother of Augustine: persuaded of the value of his soul
and grieved over his resistance to the gospel, she pursued her wandering son with her prayers and sometimes followed him physically. One
Christian from whom she sought advice encouraged her to continue
praying, saying, "It is not possible that the son of such tears should
perish."[4] In time she bore a spiritual son through her earnest tears.

Or we might consider Charles Spurgeon's faithful mother, of whom
he writes in this way:

It was the custom, on Sunday evenings, while we were yet little
children, for her to stay at home with us, and then we sat round
the table, and read verse by verse, and she explained the Scripture to us. After that was done, then came the time of pleading;
there was a little piece of Alleine's *Alarm*, or of Baxter's *Call to
the Unconverted*, and this was read with pointed observations
made to each of us as we sat round the table; and the question
was asked, how long it would be before we would think about
our state, how long before we would seek the Lord. Then came
a mother's prayer, and some of the words of that prayer we shall
never forget, even when our hair is grey. I remember, on one
occasion, her praying thus: "Now, Lord, if my children go on in
their sins, it will not be from ignorance that they perish, and my

3. Quoted in Arnold Dallimore, *George Whitefield: The Life and Times of
the Great Evangelist of the 18th Century Revival* (Edinburgh: Banner of Truth,
1970), 1:268.

4. Augustine, *The Confessions of Saint Augustine*, trans. E. M. Blaiklock (London: Hodder & Stoughton, 1983), 73.

soul must bear a swift witness against them at the day of judgment if they lay not hold of Christ." That thought of a mother's
bearing swift witness against me, pierced my conscience, and
stirred my heart.[5]

Here again in the relationship of a parent and child we find that
same blood-earnestness, that same conviction of the truth of God's
Word, that same determination to discharge one's duty to one's children faithfully and lovingly, that same persuasion of the value of a soul
and the desperate need of salvation. The foundations of the religious
life of John G. Paton, missionary to the New Hebrides (now known as
Vanuatu), were laid in similar fashion:

The "closet" was a very small apartment betwixt the other two,
having room only for a bed, a little table and a chair, with a diminutive window shedding diminutive light on the scene. This was
the Sanctuary of that cottage home. Thither daily, and often-
times a day, generally after each meal, we saw our father retire,
and "shut to the door"; and we children got to understand by a
sort of spiritual instinct (for the thing was too sacred to be talked
about) that prayers were being poured out there for us, as of old
by the High Priest within the veil in the Most Holy Place. We
occasionally heard the pathetic echoes of a trembling voice pleading as if for life, and we learned to slip out and in past that door
on tiptoe, not to disturb the holy colloquy. The outside world
might not know, but we knew, whence came that happy light as
of a new-born smile that always was dawning on my father's face:
it was a reflection from the Divine Presence, in the consciousness
of which he lived. Never, in temple or cathedral, on mountain or
in glen, can I hope to feel that the Lord God is more near, more
visibly walking and talking with men, than under that humble
cottage roof of thatch and oaken wattles. Though everything else
in religion were by some unthinkable catastrophe to be swept out
of memory, or blotted from my understanding, my soul would
wander back to those early scenes, and shut itself up once again in

<hr>

5. Charles H. Spurgeon, *Autobiography: Volume 1—The Early Years* (Edinburgh: Banner of Truth, 1962), 43–45.

that sanctuary closet, and, hearing still the echoes of those cries to God, would hurl back all doubt with the victorious appeal, "He walked with God, why may not I?"[6]

Paton's parents did not allow these things simply to lie on the surface of their children's souls, a mere awareness of things spiritual rather than reality known and felt. Rather, these parental prayers formed the basis for their direct dealing with the children for the good of their souls, as they wrestled with God for their children and then wrestled with their children for God. Paton also records how family worship was an unvarying part of life in his father's house, an occasion that proved a blessing beyond the family:

> None of us can remember that any day ever passed unhallowed thus: no hurry for market, no rush to business, no arrival of friends or guests, no trouble or sorrow, no joy or excitement, ever prevented at least our kneeling around the family altar, while the High Priest led our prayers to God, and offered himself and his children there. And blessed to others, as well as to ourselves, was the light of such example! I have heard that, in long after-years, the worst woman in the village of Torthorwald, then leading an immoral life, but since changed by the grace of God, was known to declare, that the only thing that kept her from despair and from the Hell of the suicide, was when in the dark winter nights she crept close up underneath my father's window and heard him pleading in Family Worship that God would convert "the sinner from the error of wicked ways, and polish him as a jewel for the Redeemer's crown." "I felt," said she, "that I was a burden on that good man's heart, and I knew that God would not disappoint him. That thought kept me out of Hell, and at last led me to the only Saviour."[7]

We could easily comb the pages of history to find countless further examples of Christian men and women who felt this profound

---

6. John G. Paton, *John G. Paton: Missionary to the New Hebrides* (Edinburgh: Banner of Truth, 1965), 8.

7. Paton, *John G. Paton*, 14–15.

concern, in accordance with their position and responsibilities, for those without Christ.

Failure to Communicate

Equally, we find all too many grievous illustrations of those who felt eternity far off and so could not convincingly urge men and women to flee from the wrath to come, who held so fast to the stuff of this life that they were not able to call sinners to cling to Christ alone with conviction. So we find the prophet Ezekiel complaining of those who prophesy "Peace!" when there is no peace (Ezek. 13:10, 16), assuring people—in the face of sure and impending judgment—that everything will be fine. Or we can contrast the urgency of Baxter and Bunyan with Harry Emerson Fosdick, the infamous theologically liberal preacher of the early twentieth century, marching in the vanguard of unbelief dressed in the clothes of religion. Fosdick declared that preaching is personal counseling on a group basis. Evangelists of our day preach health, wealth, and happiness, fixing the eyes of their audiences on the stuff of this life and calling them to lay up treasures on earth, making Jesus at best the way to financial security, the truth of mere self-realization or self-actualization, and the life of earthly fulfillment, so that no one can come to really love himself except by Him. The world still hears men who—claiming the authority of Christ—tell them that there is peace where there is, in reality, no true or lasting peace.

But perhaps more terrifying is the case of Lot, for the Bible tells us that Lot was a righteous man (2 Peter 2:7). Nevertheless, when Lot spoke it seems that something necessary was lacking or something damaging was present, and his message was fatally undermined. When Sodom was about to be destroyed, Lot was sent to his sons-in-law with an urgent warning of the onrushing judgment, calling upon them, "Get up, get out of this place; for the LORD will destroy this city!" What it was that undercut his message we do not know for sure, but his vital communication never reached its target: "To his sons-in-law he seemed to be joking" (Gen. 19:14). Their reaction was much like that of the audience in Søren Kierkegaard's well-known illustration: "It happened that a fire broke out backstage in a theater. The clown came out to inform the public. They thought it was a jest and applauded. He repeated his warning, they shouted even louder. So I think the world will come to an end amid general applause from all the wits, who believe that it is a joke."[8]

Eli also stands out as a stark example of failure in the parental sphere. While recorded dealings between Eli and his sons show his concern and sorrow, there is something tame and toothless about his words. This, it seems, was symptomatic of his relationship with them. When his sons were corrupting everything that was precious about the worship of God, stealing the best of the sacrifices, and having sexual relationships with the women who gathered at the entrance to the tabernacle, Eli spoke to his sons in this way: "Why do you do such things? For I hear of your evil dealings from all the people. No, my sons! For it is not a good report that I hear. You make the LORD's people transgress" (1 Sam. 2:23–25). There is truth in these words, but no cutting edge. It is hardly appropriate to hint that blasphemy and sexual immorality merely constitute something less than a good report! Evidently, God also knew something was lacking: "For I have told him that I will judge his house forever for the iniquity which he knows, because his sons made themselves vile, and he did not restrain them" (1 Sam. 3:13). Eli's feeble protestations did not count as restraint—they were too little and too late. They had no power, no bite.

Lot terrifies us not because he was an unbeliever who had no real message to bring, but because he was a righteous man who still went unheeded, who failed to communicate the need to be saved. Eli terrifies us because he was a man who served God in His tabernacle and was concerned for the glory of God, but he signally failed to promote holiness in his own family and in the nation. He failed to restrain wickedness, and his remonstrance and rebukes had no power.

David: The Brokenhearted Evangelist

So what makes the difference? What makes a Christian not only urgent, earnest, and eager to see men and women saved from their sins but also compelling and convicting? The answer lies in our own character and

---

8. Søren Kierkegaard, *Either/Or* (New York: Doubleday, 1959),1:30.

conviction, in our disposition toward and relationship to God and His truth. A repentant David demonstrates this potent spirit of the brokenhearted evangelist in Psalm 51.

As recorded in 2 Samuel 11 and 12, though King David was a man after God's own heart, he was enticed by and became enmeshed in sin. David saw Bathsheba, the wife of Uriah the Hittite, bathing one evening. He sent for her and committed adultery with her. Uriah, one of David's faithful warriors who was listed among his mighty men (2 Sam. 23:37), was battling the Ammonites at the time. David desperately tried to cover up his iniquity by calling Uriah back from the battlefield, but the soldier had too strong a sense of duty to enjoy even the legitimate joys and blessings of home while his brothers-in-arms were suffering all the dangers and privations of war. Even when David plied him with drink, Uriah held firm. In desperation, David sent Uriah back to the front carrying his own death warrant: a message for Joab, the commander of the army, ordering him to send Uriah into the hottest part of the battle and then isolate him, in order that he should be killed. Once Uriah had been slaughtered, Joab sent home a casual report, mentioning in passing that Uriah the Hittite had died. David sent back an equally casual response, and then—his hands stained with the wickedness of adultery and murder—he took Bathsheba as his wife, and in due time she gave birth to a son.

It must therefore have been for about nine months, and perhaps a little longer, that David sat on Israel's throne in a stupor of sin, unfeeling and uncaring, his conscience deadened and his heart sullen, distant from God. Then the Lord sent the prophet Nathan to the king. Nathan told David a story that stirred the native sense of justice in David's heart. Presented with the parable of a rich man who stole the delight of a poor man's heart to feed the insatiable traveler who called at his door, David condemned himself out of his own mouth: the thief must die!

We can only imagine how Nathan looked at David as he spoke those heavy words of revelation and accusation: "You are the man!" The traveler Lust had called at David's heart, and rather than satisfy himself with the rich provisions already available to him, David had stolen Uriah's wife. As God through Nathan exposed David's sin and described the coming judgment, David's sleeping conscience was roused, and he acknowledged his transgressions. Psalm 51 is the lament of David's awakened conscience, a confession of sin and a plea for mercy.

David begins the psalm with a series of repentant cries that communicate his profound sense of God's character. He is conscious of the greatness of his sins, recognizing and depending on the greatness of God's mercy:

> Have mercy upon me, O God,
>> According to Your lovingkindness;
>> According to the multitude of Your tender mercies,
>> Blot out my transgressions.
> Wash me thoroughly from my iniquity,
>> And cleanse me from my sin (vv. 1–2).

He feels the weight of God's holiness and justice and the utter wretchedness of his sinful nature and deeds. He testifies repentantly of his iniquity with a transparent and sincere shame:

> For I acknowledge my transgressions,
>> And my sin is always before me.
> Against You, You only, have I sinned,
>> And done this evil in Your sight—
>> That You may be found just when You speak,
>> And blameless when You judge.
> Behold, I was brought forth in iniquity,
>> And in sin my mother conceived me (vv. 3–5).

David is not concerned with mere externals, but he drives to the heart of the matter. God's eye penetrates to the depths of his being, and it is there that he feels his sin and his need of cleansing. His agony of soul over the horror of sin envelopes his whole humanity:

> Behold, You desire truth in the inward parts,
>> And in the hidden part You will make me to know wisdom.
> Purge me with hyssop, and I shall be clean;
>> Wash me, and I shall be whiter than snow.
> Make me hear joy and gladness,
>> That the bones You have broken may rejoice (vv. 6–8).

David returns to his central theme: his desperate desire for reconciliation with God, his sense that all is broken and that the Lord alone can restore him. David feels that all favor is gone, that he must, as it were, start afresh, and he pleads as if he were coming to God for the first time:

> Hide Your face from my sins,
>   And blot out all my iniquities.
> Create in me a clean heart, O God,
>   And renew a steadfast spirit within me.
> Do not cast me away from Your presence,
>   And do not take Your Holy Spirit from me.
> Restore to me the joy of Your salvation,
>   And uphold me by Your generous Spirit (vv. 9–12).

Humbly anticipating an experience of the rich mercy that he knows resides in the gracious heart of Almighty God, and grounded in the pleas of the previous verses, David—humbled and contrite—pours out a promise to God:

> Then I will teach transgressors Your ways,
>   And sinners shall be converted to You (v. 13).

The resolution of the thirteenth verse is built primarily upon the desires of verse 12, but with concrete piles that drive into the bedrock of all that has gone before: the profound awareness of his sin matched by his grasp of the saving mercies of a holy God, the degree to which sin offends God, his desperate need of the cleansing that only God can provide, his soul-wrenching pleas to be brought back to the favor of God. "Restore to me the joy of Your salvation, and uphold me by Your generous Spirit," David implores the Lord. And what will follow when God hears and blesses him? "Then I will teach transgressors Your ways, and sinners shall be converted to You."

This is no light, occasional, or optional work. Charles Spurgeon called this labor "the life business of the Christian."[9] Here we see the

---

9. C. H. Spurgeon, "The Christian's Great Business," in *The Metropolitan Tabernacle Pulpit* (Pasadena, Tex.: Pilgrim Publications, 2002), 19:494.

character of the brokenhearted evangelist. We hear the cry of a man conscious of his own sin, looking to God for forgiveness, and determined to live to honor and glorify the God of his salvation. Though we must each take account of our graces, gifts, and resources, this is a reality that ought to bind our consciences all our days upon earth.

Like David, we should feel this to be our undeniable obligation: *"I will* teach transgressors Your ways: I am resolved. Everything in me is bound to this. I am conscious of it as a duty. I am under conviction by the Spirit of God, whom I desire to uphold me to act in this way." David's declaration communicates a sense of compulsion. He has both a strong desire for the work and a settled purpose to undertake it. In David's language, it is the work of teaching transgressors God's ways in order that sinners might be converted to Him. In essence, it is the declaration of gospel truth to sinners in order that they might be saved.

Where We Live

We live in a fallen world. Humanity is taken up with and trapped in sin; it is our native environment, whatever our country or culture. We are slaves of sin, and transgression of God's law comes naturally. Such wickedness has fearful consequences, whether they are acknowledged or not: unrepentant sinners are exposed to the wrath and condemnation of God, liable to all miseries in this life, to death itself, and to the pains of hell forever (The Shorter Catechism, Baptist Version, Q. 20).

As we look within us, we see the filth of our own hearts and the horror of our own transgressions. As we look without, we find every nation consumed with and obsessed by filth, froth, and folly. Barriers to iniquity are eroded and removed, if ever they existed. Legislators promote godlessness on a grand scale, not just at a tangent to God's Word but utterly regardless of it. In the modern West, civil statutes that once were founded on God's moral law enshrined in the Ten Commandments are being swept away and replaced with the concoctions of the moment. The bestselling and genuinely popular media pander to an appetite for godlessness and self-indulgence. False religions—with and without the veneer of the Christian name—are on the rise, and few dare to criticize their sins and excesses. How many idol temples—outwardly and evidently religious or masquerading under the guise of stadia and shopping centers and strip clubs and other such things—are built in comparison to the number of true gospel churches established? How clear and public a testimony idolatry and carnality have in comparison with the good news of salvation through Christ Jesus the Lord!

This is not a general but distant problem. It is both particular and immediate. Consider the town and neighborhood in which you live: go out with your eyes open and observe the perversion, immorality, licentiousness, drunkenness, violence, and other gross sins that characterize our society. Walk among the men and women with influence and see the displays of license and vulgarity, following all their carnal passions and instincts, clothes clinging to flesh or simply not covering it, and pouring blasphemy and filth from their lips. Assess how rampant are those more acceptable sins at which the nations wink but which are an affront to the God of heaven and earth. Behind a veneer of respectability and a façade of morality—and sometimes the outward forms of religion—lie horrible selfishness and abandonment. Think even of the street on which you live and the real godlessness of your otherwise pleasant and friendly neighbors, living with no thought of God. Some of us might look at the members of our own families and see their sin written large.

On every side the dark is rising, a revival of iniquity that—so powerful and insistent does it seem to be—we might wish were mirrored in advancing holiness in the church of Jesus Christ. All the misery and infidelity attendant upon such a course is paraded before us. Rank godlessness rises up on every side. Satan rubs his hands with glee, and the mouth of hell yawns to receive its victims.

If you are a Christian, this is the place in which you live and the system from which you have been redeemed. You used to congregate with sinners to share in sin; wickedness was the atmosphere you breathed and transgression your way of life. Now, though, you have been plucked as a brand from the burning. This is the world of which you once had a portion and from which you have now been delivered, but it is the world in which you still live and through which you are making your pilgrimage. God has granted to you the joy of His salvation and upholds you with His generous Spirit. Do you not look with genuine compassion and profound pity on people dead in their sins and dying in sin, being consigned for all eternity to a place of endless torment and grievous condemnation? Outwardly respectable and outwardly despicable sinners alike are caught in a downward spiral that ends in the pit. And what will you do? How will you communicate the need to be saved?

Psalm 51 puts this question to the Christian in the very context of redemption from sin in a world captured by sin. We must, of course, find the solution to this question in our Bibles rather than in a sentimental knee-jerk reaction or a program built on mere pragmatism. As those aiming to be children of God without fault in the midst of a crooked and perverse generation, as those called to shine as lights in the world (Phil. 2:15), we must find and embrace God's answer to this question.

David labors under a sense of compulsion: "*I will* teach transgressors Your ways." And we must face the same obligation. Concerning this Spirit-borne sense of compulsion, we must address this question: "Am I willing?"

The Character in Which David Speaks

David was a multifaceted man with many roles and gifts. He was a king, ruling over Israel as God's anointed. He was a prophet, speaking and recording the inspired words of Psalm 51 and many others besides, the mouthpiece of the Almighty for truth and praise, both in the Psalms and in some of the sacred histories. He was a poet, the sweet singer of Israel, blessed by God to put songs of joy and gladness as well as woe and horror over sin into the mouths of God's people. He was a mighty warrior, who from his youth had snatched lambs from the mouths of lions and bears, and had slain giants. He was a gracious and tender shepherd who had looked after his father's flock, and in doing so had been equipped for the work of shepherding the people of God.

There is no doubt that David was an unusually gifted man. Most of us could not begin to hold a candle to David's sun with regard to some of his extraordinary and God-given capacities and gifts. He was a son, brother, husband, and father. He was, after the pattern of his time, a well-educated and mentally astute man, a man of genuine insight spiritually and intellectually. As far as his public pronouncements might be considered, you might even call him a preacher.

But look again at Psalm 51. Which of these characters or roles does David assume in order to write this psalm? What is the garment that he wears as he makes this declaration? While many of David's roles, traits, and gifts are evident in what he writes, or at least lie in the background, he does not express himself clothed with the mantle of any of these. None of them is prominent in this psalm. None provides the platform from which David speaks. He does not write as a king, or first and foremost as a prophet. Though he uses a poetic form, he does not write primarily as a poet. He writes not as a warrior or shepherd, nor does he parade his other qualities or roles. Rather, David presents himself here as a penitent, pardoned sinner—nothing more, nothing less, and nothing else. Everything else is abandoned, and he strips himself of everything else that we might consider a qualification for his task. He stands before us as a sinner weeping over his sins and pardoned through God's grace in Christ.

To adopt such a character provides none of us with a route of escape. We cannot excuse ourselves by saying, "Well, David was a king!" because he is not writing as a king. We cannot evade the demands of this text by pointing to his prophetic office or simply claim that he was more gifted or better educated, because those things are put aside or lie in the background. All other factors—our own roles, traits, and gifts—help to determine the sphere in which we take up the task of evangelism and the opportunities we have, but they do not allow us to avoid the holy pressure of this duty. Here is Spurgeon's advice in a sermon on Proverbs 11:30, that he who wins souls is wise:

> I have said enough, brethren, I trust, to make some of you desire to occupy the position of soul-winners: but before I further address myself to my text I should like to remind you, that the honor does not belong to ministers only; they may take their full share of it, but it belongs to every one of you who have devoted yourselves to Christ: such honor have all the saints. Every man here, every woman here, every child here, whose heart is right with God, may be a soul-winner. There is no man placed by God's providence

where he cannot do some good. There is not a glowworm under a hedge but gives a needed light; and there is not a laboring man, a suffering woman, a servant-girl, a chimney-sweeper, or a crossing-sweeper, but what has opportunities for serving God; and what I have said of soul-winners belongs not to the learned doctor of divinity, or to the eloquent preacher alone, but to you all who are in Christ Jesus. You can, each of you, if grace enable you, be thus wise, and win the happiness of turning souls to Christ through the Holy Spirit.[10]

"A Place to Occupy, a Post to Maintain"

Lest you be already overwhelmed at this prospect, let me offer a comforting caution: while I have no wish to pull any punches, the last thing I wish to do is to afflict any sensitive saint with false guilt. So, with Spurgeon, I am not suggesting that Christians in secular employment are second-class citizens of the New Jerusalem or that the *best* Christians are full-time evangelists. God has most emphatically not called every believer to be a gospel minister or evangelist in the vocational sense. Often our ideas of evangelism involve something "out there" on the spiritual equivalent of a Special Forces mission. But to think like this would be to cripple our consciences, deaden us with despair, and blind us to what lies close at hand. Listen to the eighteenth-century Particular Baptist pastor and one of the cofounders of the Baptist Missionary Society, John Sutcliff, on diligent endeavors to promote the cause of Christ:[11]

An attention to this is immediately, yet not merely, the work of ministers. While these take the lead, they ought to be seconded and supported by the vigorous efforts of all the friends of truth and holiness. Animated by the principle in our text, such will be ready to say to their ministers, as the men of Israel said to Ezra,

---

10. C. H. Spurgeon, "Soul Winning," in *The Metropolitan Tabernacle Pulpit* (Pasadena, Tex: Pilgrim Publications, 1970), 15:28.

11. John Sutcliff was one of the circle of friends that included William Carey, John Ryland Jr., and Andrew Fuller, who did much to advance the cause of Christ in their day.

when an important affair was to be undertaken, "Arise, for this matter belongeth unto thee; we also will be with thee; be of good courage and do it" [Ezra 10:4].

Having your souls enlivened by this disposition, you will each study your station and what can be done in it. You have each a place to occupy, a post to maintain. Fill up the place, make good the post where you are stationed. For instance, you who are heads of families, great is the truth reposed in your hands. Your children, your servants, claim your attention. Their health, their temporal concerns, lie near your hearts. The feelings of humanity, the dictates of natural affection, lead you thus far. But you profess to be Christians. And if your hearts are influenced by the principles of Christianity, your practice will correspond with your profession. So doing you will pay a due regard to the eternal interests of your domestics. The example of Abraham, approved by heaven, and recorded in the page of sacred history, will be admired and imitated. "I know," saith Jehovah, "that he will command his children and his household after him, and they shall keep the way of the Lord to do justice and judgment" [Genesis 18:19].

Were we to take a view of the numerous orders in human society and the distinct obligations of each in a religious view, we should carry the subject beyond the limits now assigned. Suffice it to remark that every one has a proper line in which he should walk and some peculiar privilege which should be improved. The part which every individual acts is of importance, as the smallest wheel, the minutest pin in a watch, is of consequence to the regular movement of the whole machine. Even you that are servants are repeatedly exhorted so to act "that you may adorn the doctrine of God our Saviour in all things" [Titus 2:10].[12]

---

12. John Sutcliff, "Jealousy for the Lord of Hosts Illustrated," appendix 2 in *One Heart and One Soul: John Sutcliff of Olney, His Friends and His Times* by Michael A. G. Haykin (Darlington, U.K.: Evangelical Press, 1994), 363–64. Sutcliff preached the sermon at a meeting of the Northampton Particular Baptist Association at Clipstone on April 27, 1791. I am indebted to Michael Haykin for providing me with his transcript of this sermon.

Our responsibility lies where our sovereign God has put us, in the sphere to which He has called us. It is there we are to conduct ourselves as brokenhearted evangelists and pursue our calling as Christians, embracing our vocation—whatever it may be—as those who desire and intend to make Christ known to others. If He calls us to something more definite and all-consuming (and I trust that you will at least consider whether that might be the case, guided by the Word of God and the church of Christ and trusted, insightful counselors), well and good, but if He does not, let us serve Him where we are. Let no exhausted mother, with her hands full of home and children, bruise her soul with the conviction either that she has no way of serving Christ in this way or that she is somehow prevented by her children and her home from doing something worthwhile. Rather, that is the very sphere of her labor. Her mission field is at her feet (and quite possibly under them and in her arms and on her back and currently drawing something indelible on something irreplaceable). Indeed, for her to feel falsely guilty about what she is not doing or to transfer that guilt to her children in resentment and bitterness will only prevent the good that she is called to do as a minister to her children. Consider some of the earlier examples of Augustine, Spurgeon, and Paton, to name but three. We tend to look at those men and think that they are the evangelists, but each of them was first evangelized by his own parents.

Let no man who has no gift for public speech berate himself for not being a preacher. Let him rather consider what he might do as a friend who draws alongside others in any number of contexts. The husband who labors countless hours in the week to put bread on the table for his wife and any children God might give may not be able to spend every Saturday visiting friends, handing out tracts, or knocking on doors, but he might be able to remember in prayer those who do and perhaps give an hour or so once a month to such endeavors.

There are countless avenues—perhaps not public, not formalized, not extravagant—by means of which the people of God can righteously manufacture or embrace an opportunity to declare the truth concerning the Lord Christ. In fifteenth-century England, a humble scholar by the name of Thomas Bilney became a true Christian. He heard an

arrogant and aggressive fellow-student at Cambridge publicly attack
Philip Melanchthon's teachings. Bilney devised a subtle means of telling that student the truth. He asked if he could make a confession to
the student in question, who agreed, and later recorded the encounter
in this way:

> Here I have occasion to tell you a story which happened at
> Cambridge. Master Bilney, or rather Saint Bilney, that suffered
> death for God's word sake; the same Bilney was the instrument
> whereby God called me to knowledge; for I may thank him, next
> to God, for that knowledge that I have in the word of God. For
> I was as obstinate a papist as any was in England, insomuch that
> when I should be made bachelor of divinity, my whole oration
> went against Philip Melancthon and against his opinions. Bilney
> heard me at that time, and perceived that I was zealous without
> knowledge: and he came to me afterward in my study, and desired
> me, for God's sake, to hear his confession. I did so; and, to say the
> truth, by his confession I learned more than before in many years.
> So from that time forward I began to smell the word of God, and
> forsook the school-doctors and such fooleries. Now, after I had
> been acquainted with him, I went with him to visit the prisoners
> in the tower at Cambridge; for he was ever visiting prisoners, and
> sick folk. So we went together, and exhorted them as well as we
> were able to do; moving them to patience, and to acknowledge
> their faults.[13]

The fiery aggressor and subsequently vigorous convert was Hugh
Latimer, who, as an old man, was also to die a martyr's death, testifying
to the sole, saving sufficiency of the Lord Christ. But you will notice
how Bilney, who had a strong desire to declare and defend the truth,
was quite prepared to use various and appropriate means to bring the
gospel to bear. Bilney was physically small and weak, constitutionally
frail, and socially reticent. One historian describes him thus: "Timid
and retiring, his influence was exerted in secret; he never appeared as
a public teacher of the new system [Luther's recovery of the gospel],

---

13. Hugh Latimer, "The First Sermon on the Lord's Prayer," in *Sermons by
Hugh Latimer* (Cambridge: Cambridge University Press, 1844), 1:334–35.

but, in private intercourse with his friends, he talked to them of life and hope."[14] The robust and vocal Latimer might have pulled him apart in debate, but Bilney went and "made confession," and so Latimer was won. Notice, too, how Bilney "was ever visiting prisoners, and sick folk": he found his sphere, and there he served his God well and fruitfully. His constitution and character and calling did not hinder his service, but they did direct it.

So by all means be galvanized. By all means look further afield. By all means be inventive. By all means make sacrifices for the sake of Christ and the lost. But by no means reproach yourselves for things that are not sin in you, even though they may be sin in another. Robert Candlish, a nineteenth-century preacher and writer from Scotland, gives some good advice:

> The opening of the lips must be the same for all and in all. But the manner of the mouth's showing forth God's praise may be infinitely varied. Constitution and circumstances, temper, time, talents, opportunities; all must be taken into the reckoning. No martinet or formal rule can be laid down. None may prescribe to his brother. None may judge his brother. Every one acts for himself. Only let every one,—all the more for this discretionary allowance,—be sure that his eye is single; that when he offers the prayer, "Open thou my lips," and awaits the reply, it is really that "his mouth may show forth God's praise."[15]

But if your particular calling *is* to preach the gospel, then woe to you if you fail to do so (1 Cor. 9:16). As Sutcliff says, let ministers "take the lead"; gospel preachers are to be at the vanguard of gospel advance. If anyone ought to be on the front line, they ought to be, not just within the safe confines of an appointed meeting place or within the enclosed moments of an appointed meeting time, but constantly seeking for and carving out and taking on opportunities. We cannot do it alone, and

---

14. R. Demaus, *Hugh Latimer: A Biography* (London: Religious Tract Society, 1881), 23.

15. Robert Candlish, *The Prayer of a Broken Heart* (Edinburgh: Adam and Charles Black, 1873), 84–85.

we long for the practical and prayerful support of healthy saints, but we must put our hand to the plough.

Taking all this into account, as well as your distinctive calling, particular constitution, or specific character, consider that the root and foundation of your obligation to teach transgressors the ways of God—the issue of whether you are to be a witness to God's grace, teaching transgressors the ways of Jehovah—lies in whether you are a repentant and pardoned sinner. If you and I are such pardoned sinners, having come with tears of genuine sorrow and received forgiveness of our sins from God, then we lie under the same obligation as David. Indeed, there is a sense in which we are beyond David, prophet though he was. God has revealed Himself in the new covenant, through the person and work of Christ, with a clarity, glory, and beauty not seen before. He has shown not just the loveliness of His power and justice but has also thrown into yet brighter relief His goodness, mercy, and truth. These glories bind us even more to make known to those dead in trespasses and sins God's ways of goodness, mercy, justice, punishment, forgiveness, righteousness, holiness, and peace. We too ought to possess this strong desire and settled purpose to be a teacher of God's ways to transgressors. This verse demands that everybody professing to be a pardoned, penitent sinner be a new-covenant evangelist. Archibald Alexander allows no evasion:

> In the charter which Christ gave to his disciples, who formed the first church under the new dispensation, the first command is one which requires action. "Go," says he. Every Christian must be on the alert. He has marching orders from the Captain of his salvation. He cannot sit down in ease and idleness, and yet be a Christian. As the father said to his son in the parable, "Go, work in my vineyard," so Christ says to every disciple; and it will not answer to say, "I go, sir," and yet refuse obedience. We must be *doers* of the word, and not mere hearers. We must be doers of the word, and not mere professors [those making a profession]. The command given by the risen Saviour is still in force, and as it was obligatory on all who heard it at first, so it is binding on all who hear it now. "Go."

But what are we to do? *"Proselyte."* Make disciples. Convert to Christianity. The very word "proselyte" will frighten some people. No heresy in their view is so great as sectarism. But Christianity is so intolerant, that it will bear no other religion; it seeks to overthrow every other system. If it would have admitted the claims of other religions, it would have escaped persecution. But no; it denounced every other system and mode of worship as hateful to God, and destructive to the soul. And it made every disciple a *proselyter.* And every one now, whether male or female, bond or free, Jew or Greek, who professes Christianity, takes upon himself or herself the obligation to convert others to Christianity.[16]

The commentator Matthew Henry also declared that "penitents should be preachers"[17]—that is, repentant sinners obtaining peace ought to pass on their hope to others. He means this not necessarily in the formal, public sense, but most certainly in the sense and character in which David speaks in Psalm 51:13. We ought all to feel an obligation—a strong and settled desire and purpose, an overwhelming conviction and resolve—to teach transgressors the ways of God. We should feel the duty and privilege of being the one to bring truth to the ungodly. If we name the name of Christ, we ought to have something of this desire. We are saved to be instruments of God's glory, and as such we are obliged and made willing to declare all His works to sinners, that they might be converted:

> The first impulse of the restored penitent, when the case as between him and his God is settled, is to go forth from his closet, the secret place of his God,—where the covenant of peace through atoning blood has been ratified as a personal transaction,—and tell what great things the Lord has done. That should and must be your immediate instinct. Many motives may prompt such action. You long to give vent to your emotions; and it is a relief to you to impart to others your sorrows and your joys; your late dismal

---

16. Archibald Alexander, "Christianity in Its Nature Aggressive," in *Practical Truths* (Harrisonburg, Va.: Sprinkle Publications, 1998), 32–33.

17. Matthew Henry, *Job to Song of Solomon*, vol. 3 of *Commentary on the Whole Bible* (Peabody, Mass.: Hendrickson, 1991), 354.

fears, and your present blessed hopes. There is pleasure also in the communication of good tidings. And surely there is an earnest and eager desire to save the lost. For you cannot, if you yourselves are taken from the horrible pit, look with indifference on the state of your companions who are still sinking unconsciously in its miry clay.

But over and above all these, there is a paramount consideration. It is the conviction that you owe it to the "God of your salvation" to "show forth his praise."[18]

Are you willing? This is not a matter of whether you feel like it. Desire is not just a matter of whether you have some instinctive inclination or if your emotions happen to be raised to the right pitch. We need a binding resolution of conscience compelling each of us. Each of us must have the conviction that we stand before God as saved sinners who—on the basis of our own pardon—lie under an undeniable obligation to exercise the glorious privilege of presenting Christ to a transgressing, fallen generation. It is in this character that David speaks. Insofar as we possess that character, we lie under the same obligation.

The Nature of the Task

What is the work to which we are called? While we shall go on to consider this in greater depth, we can glean at least two things from the surface of David's declaration.

A Deeply Personal Task

David says, "*I will*": this is a personal undertaking. Do you pray for the men who stand to preach in your church—and elsewhere—pleading with God for a blessing upon the work? Good—there will be no success without it! Do you support the church with cheerful generosity, financially and in other ways, so that your local congregation and others might spread the gospel? Excellent—much to be commended! Do you encourage others who engage in this work, drawing alongside truehearted brothers and sisters, assuring them of your prayers and

---

18. Candlish, *Prayer of a Broken Heart*, 88–89.

concern for them? Praise God—much to be appreciated! But what do *you* actually *do*?

Do you personally exercise your particular obligation and privilege to teach transgressors God's ways? What do you do over and above those things just mentioned? Prayer, giving, and encouragement, as well as hospitality, enable us to enter into the work of others (3 John 8). But David is not speaking in that way here. He is saying, "I personally will teach transgressors your ways." This work is not something carried out by one, two, or a few people. This is not a spectator sport, nor is it bounded by the physical limits of the pulpit. It is not something carried out by a few particularly keen or overly enthusiastic or even strangely deluded individuals. This is the work of the entire redeemed church of Jesus Christ—and not just collectively.

Again, listen to Andrew Fuller and John Sutcliff, whose hearts burned with a desire for the glory of God and compassion for the lost. Here is Fuller:

> The primitive churches were not mere assemblies of men who agreed to meet together once or twice a week, and to subscribe for the support of an accomplished man who should on those occasions deliver lectures on religion. They were men gathered out of the world by the preaching of the cross, and formed into society for the promotion of Christ's kingdom in their own souls and in the world around them. It was not the concern of the ministers or elders only; the body of the people were interested in all that was done, and, according to their several abilities and stations, took part in it. Neither were they assemblies of heady, high-minded, contentious people, meeting together to argue on points of doctrine or discipline, and converting the worship of God into scenes of strife. They spoke the truth; but it was in love; they observed discipline; but, like an army of chosen men, it was that they might attack the kingdom of Satan to greater advantage. Happy were it for our churches if we could come to a closer imitation of this model![19]

And here is more of Sutcliff:

---

19. Andrew Fuller, "The Pastor's Address to His Christian Hearers,

James addressed his epistle to those what were "scattered abroad" (James 1:1). This is the common lot of God's people. Certainly it is to answer some wise end in the general plan of divine providence. Nor is it perhaps hard to determine what this may be. Are they not the salt of the earth (see Matthew 5:13)? It is not proper that the salt should lie all in one heap. It should be scattered abroad. Are they not the light of the world (see Matthew 5:14)? These taken collectively should, like the sun, endeavour to enlighten the whole earth. As all the rays, however, that each can emit are limited in their extent, let them be dispersed that thus the whole globe may be illuminated. Are they not witnesses for God? It is necessary they be distributed upon every hill and every mountain, in order that their sound may go into all the earth and their words unto the ends of the world (see Psalm 19:4).[20]

Each one of us who professes Christ needs to be personally engaged in the work in accordance with our calling and opportunity. This is your role and privilege, your obligation and mine, as individual Christians. Our vocation, whatever it might be, might govern the opportunities, places, and times at which we might be able to fulfill this obligation, but each one individually is under the obligation. Few indeed are those individuals who do not have or cannot make some opportunities to engage in this work: Paul was the means of converting the soldiers chained to him in a Roman prison. Is it possible that we might be cut off from all opportunities? Yes, but there will be few reading this who do not have, or—with biblical ingenuity and determination, like Thomas Bilney— cannot make opportunities to engage in such a calling. Carry this away with you: you, as an individual Christian, are under this obligation. It is your personal task to tell people the good news.

A Deeply Humbling Task
David was a great man in many ways, yet he assumes none of the trappings of greatness for the purpose of writing this psalm and making this

Entreating Their Assistance in Promoting the Interest of Christ," in *The Complete Works of Andrew Fuller* (Harrisonburg, Va.: Sprinkle Publications, 1988), 3:346.
20. Sutcliff, "Jealousy for the Lord of Hosts Illustrated," 364.

declaration. He does not say, "I am a king, so hear me! I am a prophet, so regard my word! I am a poet, so let my words tickle your ears until you are persuaded!" No, David speaks to us in the garb of a pardoned sinner, and that qualifies and situates him for the work. Had he come in another character, speaking down the years from a different time, place, and culture, we would have many excuses by which to begin shaving off the edges of our response as sinners and our responsibility as saints. But David comes in a universal condition, as a sinner. He comes in a position granted by the grace of God, as a sinner saved from his sins. We should pretend to be nothing more than this when we bring the truth of God to bear upon the lives and consciences of transgressors.

Pretend to be anything more than this, and you are finished before you start. If we come puffed up and pompous with what we are beyond being sinners saved by grace—"I am such-and-such a great one, therefore listen to me!"—then we might as well zip our mouths shut on the spot. Although we will deal with this in more detail further on, be persuaded that you cannot go to another wretched, sinning creature clad in the imagined pomposity of high calling, dignified profession, public position, accumulated wealth, church office, or anything else, and then unload pretentious drivel from a position of illusory moral or social superiority. You must come as a sinner to sinners and speak to them of the pardon that you have obtained, and that is a humbling posture. It punctures all our pride and pomposity. Nineteenth-century preacher William M. Taylor illustrates this approach:

> I have somewhere read of a hardened criminal who was condemned to die and waiting for execution. Christian people were deeply interested in him and wished for his salvation. Pastors of different churches visited him and talked with him and prayed with him. But all they did and said seemed only to harden him the more, for they never got near him. They were afraid of him. They never touched him. At length, they bethought themselves of a member of the community, known of all men for his holiness and tenderness and wisdom in the winning of souls, and they got him to visit him. When he entered the condemned cell, he sat down beside the prisoner, by whom also he was well known, and told him the simple story of the cross, and when he had finished

it, he laid his hand upon the criminal's shoulder and said to him with a look of inexpressible emotion: "Now wasn't it a great sacrifice for the Son of God to lay down his life for guilty sinners like me and you?" In a moment the fountains of the great deep were broken up. The heart of the man was touched. The big tears ran down his cheeks, and the bursting sobs seemed to convulse his frame. From that time he was a different man, and listened with interest to all that was said to him, while ever and anon he would exclaim, "To think of such a good and holy man, as I know him to be, putting himself on a level with me, and saying 'Sinners like me and you'!"[21]

Put yourself, then, on a level with other people and say, "Sinners like me and you." Present yourself as anything else, and they may be offended by something other than the gospel. Come as anything but a sinner who has received grace from the God of heaven and earth, and people will turn away from you. Instead, you should present yourself as you are when you are alone before God on your knees, as you will be on the Day of Judgment. Nothing else will matter on that day but that you are a pardoned sinner. When we are stripped of all the insulating pomposity and pride that other things too readily provide and to which we too readily cling, then we are best situated and truly qualified to draw alongside any other sinner.

Parents, how do you deal with your children? Do you try to hide the fact that you are a pardoned sinner? How do you deal with your friends? Do you come to them as a suited and booted Christian from a worthy church with a mass of pretended superiority—or as a pardoned sinner? With your colleagues at work, are you sufficiently persuaded of the reality of this obligation that you are willing to ditch your professional pride and speak to them, when opportunity provides, as a pardoned sinner? That is the basis on which you can open your mouth to any person. This wins the ear. When you come to sinners as a sinner and profess that grace alone has changed you, the door opens more

---

21. William M. Taylor, "The Cleansing of the Leper," in *The Miracles of Our Saviour* (New York: Hodder & Stoughton, 1890), 119–20.

surely. That does not mean that we parade all our past sins, drawing out of our souls all the filth of previous experience. It does mean that we must climb down and acknowledge the reality of what we are before God. That is deeply humbling. We must get rid of all the baggage and insulation that keep other sinners at arm's length from us, the things that keep us at arm's length from other sinners. We need to drop our guard, get in close, pretend to be nothing more than we are, and speak to men the truth as it is in Jesus.

What Is at Stake?

What is on the line as we consider our undeniable obligation to teach the gospel to every creature? What are some of the holy pressures that carry us from being brokenhearted over our own sin to being broken-hearted evangelists?

The Reality of Our Own Experience of Salvation
Only an unusual child who has been given some great gift is able to keep the news, enjoyment, and display of that gift to himself. The first desire of most children who receive a new bike for their birthday is to go out (no matter what time of day it is or how dark and cold it may be outside) and barrel up and down some portion of the road outside (no matter how short that portion may be) just to get to grips with that gift. You can be sure that they will take their gift to their friends; their joy is not full unless it has been shared. The reality of their experience of receiving is manifested by the way in which they display that gift and their gratitude for it, to anybody and everybody whom they can reach.

In the same way, every Christian has received an unspeakably great gift. You have had bestowed upon you, by God's sovereign grace and unbidden mercy in Christ, a gift the greatness and goodness of which you could not fully express if you had a thousand millennia in which to do so. Do you know and feel the blessedness of sins forgiven, the joy of having had your transgressions blotted out, the rejoicing of having the record of your sins before God's eyes utterly done away with through the blood of Jesus Christ? Is that your experience, and do you have nothing to say? Will you know nothing of the excitement of sharing what you have received with someone else?

Let us fear that if we truly have nothing to say, it might be because we have nothing real about which to speak. If you can live entirely mute, then you need to ask yourself whether you are truly saved. If you can live mute, then you need to ask yourself whether you have begun to understand even the first and most basic things about the salvation that is in Jesus Christ. If you can live mute concerning the glorious gift of salvation that you have received through Jesus Christ and Him crucified, then shame on you and me and your church and any professing Christian who claims to have received the most glorious gift that anyone could ever receive and can hide it away and say not a word about it. David's sin was public; his repentance and the fruits of his restoration would also be public. His declaration of God's ways was a testimony of truth, but also a testimony to personal experience of that truth in action. He had come to know the blessings of the man whose transgression is forgiven, whose sin is covered, whose iniquity has not been imputed to him (Ps. 32:1–2), and he wanted others to know of the blessings to be found in turning from sin to God. If this had been mere emotional excitement rather than a profound and substantial spiritual transaction, if would have produced no lasting fruit. If we say nothing, it calls into question the reality, or at the very least the depth, of our saving experience of the blood of Jesus Christ.

The Christian's Spiritual Well-Being and Joy

Consider Spurgeon's sobering words as he reflects on his experience: "I believe that the not seeking to win souls brings many spiritual maladies upon Christian men.... God in discipline often brings sorrow upon his own people because of their unholy silence as to gracious things."[22] Why discipline? Because our duty is to proclaim the praises of God, who called us "out of darkness into His marvelous light" (1 Peter 2:9), and a failure to do it is disobedience that needs to be corrected. That should hit us in the pit of our stomachs. Might it be that some of our

---

22. Spurgeon, "Christian's Great Business," 499.

individual and corporate sufferings are God's discipline because of our unholy silence as to gracious things? If we hold our tongues while a world around us parades its way to hell, then God may bring His discipline upon us. The Lord of heaven may inflict upon us—and perhaps, we must say when we look at the condition of the church in many places of the world, *is* inflicting upon us—many spiritual maladies because we are not honing the truth we know and love in the battle against ungodliness. This is not just a negative point; there is positive spiritual well-being and joy in the work of evangelism. Sutcliff, again, concurs:

> Yes, brethren, this divine temper would eminently tend to promote your own comfort. It will inspire your minds with a holy cheerfulness amidst all your labours and toils. Numerous discouragements that now damp your spirits would never be felt. Activity and pleasure would here be found united. The lukewarm professor may drag on, but like Pharaoh's chariots when the wheels were off, it will be heavily; while the vigorous, the active follower of Jesus, mounts upon the wings of eagles and, as he ascends, sings the songs of seraphs. It will tend to make happy all the friends of God around you. These beholding your heavenly ardour will be filled with holy joy.[23]

How do we keep our prayers fiery? By engaging in hand-to-hand combat with Satan's hosts, for those who are yet under his dominion. Why do we keep our spiritual weapons sharp? So that we can fight. How do we learn how to use those weapons? When we engage with lost men. Where are our graces brought to their highest pitch and exercised to their greatest degree? It is often when we are locked in mortal combat for the salvation of a soul. Where are our minds fired with holy truth so that we begin to understand, to press, and to be in earnest? When are our hearts most ablaze with love for Jesus Christ? When, in short, are we most alive as Christians? With the possible exception of the gatherings of the saints for worshiping God, it is when we are involved in the life business of the redeemed men and women of Jesus Christ, engaging with transgressors and seeking their salvation for the glory of

---

23. Sutcliff, "Jealousy for the Lord of Hosts Illustrated," 364.

God in Jesus Christ. There is little that so elevates us—that so engages the totality of our redeemed humanity—as the holy cut and thrust of evangelism. Nothing so casts us upon the grace of God in Jesus Christ. Nothing so reminds us of our need and sends us in desperation to God for increased measures of His Spirit as the reality of wrestling for souls.

David's restoration to a close walk with God would have been both manifest in and maintained by this activity. The evidence of his steadfast spirit renewed and the presence of the Spirit of God lay in these very things. The brokenhearted evangelist reminds himself of the blessings of salvation and keeps them precious in his conscience as he speaks to others who need them. His heart is blessed in the demonstration of his blessings to others.

Has it ever been your privilege to be at the birth of a new Christian? Have you ever been the one to whom someone has come days, weeks, even months or years later and said, "Did you know how God used you in my salvation?" Surely our hearts leap for joy under such circumstances! Do you want to cut yourself off from the joy of being a coworker with God? That is at stake if you deny your undeniable obligation.

The Sincerity of Our Prayers

"Your kingdom come. Your will be done on earth as it is in heaven" (Matt. 6:10). What are those but empty and meaningless words if there is no correspondent striving that God's kingdom will, in fact, come? We need to ask ourselves whether our words and deeds keep pace with our prayers.

Imagine that the next prayer meeting in your church comes round. You suddenly find that your tongue is selectively disengaged: you cannot pray about things that you have not pursued and will not actively pursue. If you could plead for conversions only if you had a clear conscience about teaching some needy person God's ways during the previous seven days, how often would you be able to pray for sinners to be saved? If you were able to bow your head before God and ask for the conversion of your neighbors only after you had begun to witness to them, how often would you pray for your neighbors? If you were given opportunities to pray for friends, colleagues, or family members only on the basis of having spoken to them of Christ, would you ever be able to pray for them? We pray publicly, I hope, for the salvation of sinners with holy earnestness, regularity, and consistency, but are our deeds keeping pace with our words? Our prayers are mere hypocrisy if they are not supported by our actions. The eloquence, length, fervency, earnestness, and consistency of our praying are not the issue. We may be pleading with God for the salvation of sinners in private as well as in public. But when we ask for something that we never strive to accomplish—perhaps have no intention of pursuing as appropriate—it renders what we have said mere emptiness. If nothing else, what would you have thought of the sincerity of David's prayers for forgiveness if his promise to speak of God's ways to sinners had proved empty?

What is at stake? The very sincerity of the petitions that we offer up to God! We can undo those prayers by our own failure to follow through in accordance with what we have sought. The answer, of course, is not to cease praying but to continue praying and start serving. While Moses held up his hand on the mountain, Joshua fought the Amalekites in the valley (Ex. 17). Like them, we need prayer on the mountains as well as combat in the valleys. Remember how our Lord, looking out on the plentiful harvest, called upon His disciples to pray that the Lord of the harvest would send out laborers (Matt. 9:37–38). We presume that they obeyed, and then He called the disciples together and sent out the Twelve as a partial answer to their own prayers (Matt. 10:1). There is no fruit from either the preaching or the praying alone; we must preach and pray, pray and preach. The two must go hand in hand.

The Health of Christ's Church

It is too easy to assume a bunker mentality with regard to the local church. We try to keep the world at bay and perhaps assume that within the hermetically sealed confines of the congregation we can preserve ourselves intact without needing to come into contact with the world. But we cannot breed Christians by natural means. Not only is there no guarantee that any family—no matter how young or healthy—will have children, but there is no guarantee that those children will become Christians, irrespective of the great and glorious privileges of being born and bred in Christian homes and raised in a gospel church. We cannot fill the church through a breeding program, and God has not called us to do so. Neither will we see the church grow as it should through ready-packaged Christians simply wandering in one day to fill the pews. We should pray that God would strengthen our hands. We should pray for the conversion of our children and should labor with every righteous means available to see them saved. We should be legitimately attractive to hungry sheep coming into our congregations seeking food for their souls.

However, if the church of Christ is to survive and thrive, if there is to be a gospel witness in the places where God has put us through many decades yet to come, if there are to be faithful men and women who will carry the torch when we have gone, then it will only be as we preach Christ and Him crucified beyond the nice, safe confines of our own families and the four walls of a church building. If we want our churches to be faithful, thriving, growing churches, it must happen through the conversion of sinners. That will come to pass only insofar as you and I undertake our undeniable obligation to teach transgressors God's ways—with all the challenges that entails and with all the problems it will bring as men and women come in with the splendid germ of the reality of redemption in their hearts, together with all their worldly baggage, the clutter of false religion, or the dross of a merely nominal Christianity, of truths misunderstood and wrongly applied. Nevertheless, the primary means by which our churches will be sustained through time is Jesus Christ's using our efforts to teach transgressors God's ways and His blessing those endeavors. Do you have a desire for the long-term good of the church of which Christ has made you a member? Do you have a commitment to the church's witness to Christ, not just in your generation but for years to come? That witness is at stake with regard to this undeniable obligation. There is a gospel chain that ties each generation of Christians to those who have gone before. The gospel advances as sinners saved by grace tell others what great things the Lord has done for them and how He has had compassion on them (Mark 5:19), and they in turn find the joy of sins forgiven and embrace the same privilege.

Our Obedience to God

It is not a sin for most of us to be something other than a preacher or missionary. The question with regard to our obedience is this: In the sphere to which God has appointed you (in consideration of your calling, circumstances, gifts, and graces), are you prepared to speak a word for Jesus Christ? If you are not, it is sin. It is sin to keep silent when those around us are dying. None of us should imagine that we are so curtailed or crippled by circumstance or calling that we cannot fulfill this obligation to be a witness. What are you thinking even now? Are you trying to ignore the reality of these things? Are excuses beginning to mount up in your brain? Are you thinking that you are the exception to the general rule that applies to everyone else, or how particular circumstances in your life somehow remove this obligation from you? Are you trying to slope your shoulders?

I do not assume that you are doing any of those things, but that is how we often react when something hard is brought to bear upon us. We hear a sermon in which the preacher makes plain some gospel duty: "This is the way of following Christ, though it is hard and costly." Most of us can generally think in a few minutes of several reasons why such a requirement should not or does not apply to us. But this is an undeniable obligation, a matter of simple and clear submission to God. How would we expect disobedience to be blessed in any other sphere? Why would we expect it to be blessed in this? It is a matter of obedience, and the Christian is a rebel who has been made a child of God. You see David in Psalm 51 offering a complete re-consecration of himself, body and soul, to God. Such is the desire of every truly saved sinner, and part of that consecration includes a readiness to speak of Jesus.

The Souls of the Unsaved

David had set a terrible example of iniquity to watching Israel. How many might have used great David, the man after God's own heart, to excuse their own transgressions? To be sure, there is in David's experience—as there is in the experience of Manasseh (2 Chron. 33) and the apostle Paul (1 Tim. 1:12–17)—a testimony to the freeness and fullness of God's forgiveness, but never as a means to indulge in sin. But what of those who would turn David's crime into a mere salve to their own conscience as they indulged their lusts, with all the fearful consequences? David wanted his hands to be free from blood (Ps. 51:14), not only the bloodguiltiness of his wicked crimes directly but also from the associated guilt of his example. He wanted to be an example of repentance, an example of mercy, an example of the way back to God.

Some of the most fervent Christians are those who have been ringleaders in iniquity before their conversion. John Bunyan was such a man, a byword for vice and godlessness in his own circle before God humbled him and turned him into the path of righteousness. Bunyan's heart was stirred, among other things, by the recognition that he had an obligation to testify as much to the eternal joys of salvation as he ever had to the passing pleasures of sin. Have you been the means of leading others astray? Have you been an example of wickedness? Have you mocked others seeking peace before seeking and finding peace yourself? Perhaps you once bore the name or reputation of a Christian while living a life marked by ungodliness and only later came to understand and enjoy a true relationship with God in Christ. It may be that you have lived your Christian life at low ebb and that you have to this point neglected those around you, men and women and children from whom you have withheld the word of life by your negligence and lukewarmness.

Surely the time has come for you to prove yourself as much a friend to the souls of men and women as you have ever been their enemy. Now is the time to cry to the Lord for mercy for your guilt and to vow—God helping you—that you will die without the blood of men and women on your hands.

Furthermore, doesn't the clear biblical teaching of hell demand that every one of us be a witness to the ungodly? Consider what the Scriptures have to say about hell. Consider that the pictures and representations of hell are symbols and shadows of a reality, and symbols and shadows are necessarily less real, less gripping, less intense than the reality that they represent. If hell is a place where the fire is not quenched and the worm always gnaws (Mark 9:43–48); a place of weeping and gnashing of teeth (Matt. 13:42, 50; Luke 13:28); of extreme and outer darkness (Matt. 25:30); of fire (Matt. 5:22; 18:9) and torment (Luke 16:28; Rev. 14:11) and condemnation (Matt. 23:33; John 5:29); if hell is the least part of what it is presented to be in God's holy Word, through those Spirit-inspired Scriptures, then *how* in the name and for the sake of our own humanity, let alone our Christian duty, could we ever remain silent about the truth that saves from hell? Is it not a simple case of charity over and above any other consideration?

Suppose that you were there when the gates of the concentration camps opened at Belsen, Dachau, or Auschwitz. Suppose that you were there in the extreme north of Russia during the depths of the Communist era, in the Kolyma Peninsula, and the gates swung out, and some of the wretched inmates of the camps shambled down upon you. What if you were there with a basket full of bread, and you held it all to your chest and would not give a single bite to one of those starving, emaciated human beings? There would almost be grounds to have you charged on the spot with murder and have your bread distributed in healthy proportion to the starving hundreds, that they might taste and live. You must be exceedingly careful in giving nutritious food to those who have been physically deprived, but you do not need to be so careful with the spiritually starving. While you may need to feed them gospel milk before you give them gospel meat, you can nevertheless call upon them to glut themselves at the gospel table, to taste and see that the Lord is good. And would you look around us, at the reality of men and women emaciated and deprived of true spiritual nourishment, while you have baskets of the bread of life in your hands, and never offer them a single bite?

Can you see God's merciful warnings painted in graphic colors along the road to hell, hear His gracious invitations to life in Christ, and watch people walking cheerfully, blindly, and deafly toward their eternal condemnation, and not call out to enforce those warnings and explain those invitations? At least the ungodly and idolaters seek to press upon others their own perversions; at least they have the sincerity to speak what they believe. Again, Spurgeon says that there are some who believe, but they tremble at the truth and never say a word. They are called demons. If we believe, tremble at the truth, and yet withhold the saving news of life in Jesus Christ for those who are now dead in their trespasses and sins, that effectively puts us in the company of demons.[24]

Your humanity is at stake; the souls of the unsaved are at stake. The sinner saved by grace is not only a person who is heartbroken over his own sins, but he is also heartbroken over the sins and present destiny of those around him (Ps. 119:136). Paul wrote weeping of those who were the enemies of the cross of Christ (Phil. 3:18). When you sit around your kitchen table with your children or your siblings or your parents, when you spend time with your friends, when you go into your office, when you walk the streets of your town, when you stand in a great concourse of men and women with the hordes thronging about you, you are in most cases seeing a mass of untaught and hell-bound sinners. Your soul should be stirred to its depths by the reality of those whom you love and even those whom you do not know, lost and on their way to an eternity under the just judgment of a holy God who will yet save whoever turns to Him:

> I think of my fellow-sinners; my companions in crime and guilt. I would fain make some suitable amends to them. And what can be more appropriate in that view than the resolution, with reference to them, and all my fellow men,—"I will teach transgressors thy ways, and sinners shall be converted to thee" (ver. 13). This is, and should be,—it must be,—the immediate and instinctive purpose of one who has himself known the ways of God, so as to be himself converted to him. Can any one who has really been thus taught and thus changed, refrain from the cry,—"Come and hear, all ye that fear God, and I will declare what he hath done for my soul?" Can he even be content with such audience, meet and few? Will he not, moved by his own experience, feel his heart burn within him for souls not fearing God; souls all but perishing? Have I been snatched as a brand from the burning? And can I resist the imperative impulse to sound a general alarm? Have I discovered the hidden treasure; gained the pearl of great price?... This is the force [of the connection].... It simply implies these two things—*first*, that it is only such experience of the Lord's gracious

---

24. Spurgeon, "Christian's Great Business," 501.

dealing with me personally, that can make it possible for me to enter upon any course of dealing, in like manner, personally, with any of my fellow-creatures and fellow-sinners around me; and *secondly*, that if I have experienced such personal dealing with me on the part of God, I cannot but try to bring it to bear on all within my reach.[25]

These things demand not only that we accept the opportunities that God gives us but also that we seek and labor for every opportunity we can find, in order to do good—ultimate good—to those who are dead in their sins.

The Honor of Jesus Christ

David cries out to God with profound insight, "Purge me with hyssop, and I shall be clean; wash me, and I shall be whiter than snow" (Ps. 51:7). David uses the language of sacrifice but applies it to the depths of his being. He deals with sins that found no direct counterpart in the sacrificial rituals of Israel, and yet still he pleads for the spiritual realities prefigured by those ceremonies. David is looking for something deeper, more powerful: he is pleading the reality that casts its shadow back through the Old Testament. David is reaching toward Messiah, the Son of God who comes into the world to save sinners.

Listen to Jesus Christ as He pleads with the Father that all those who have been given to Him shall come to Him, that He might have them all with Him where He is (John 17:24). For a moment, look to where He lies, pressed to the ground in Gethsemane, sweating great drops of blood as He embraces the Father's will in redemption. See Him expiring for sinners at Calvary. There He is with His thorn-crowned brow, with His nail-pierced hands and feet, with the flesh torn from His back. There He is being made a curse, being made sin for us, receiving in Himself the awful punishment that the sins of His people deserve. There He is, engaged in the great work of suffering and dying as an atoning sacrifice for sinners. Will you look at Christ in all the gore, filth, and agony of His death upon the cross and tell Him that

---

25. Candlish, *Prayer of a Broken Heart*, 65–66.

you have nothing to say to the ungodly? That the Christ who died to save sinners, who came not to call the righteous but sinners to repentance, is a Christ of whom you can say nothing to a sinner who will die without Him? This is the one who, as it were, holds up His wounded hands before you and says, "For My sake, and the gospel's—go! I am the Christ to whom all authority has been given in heaven and on earth; as you go, therefore, make disciples." He shows you in His hands, feet, and side and on His brow and in the depths of His eyes the tokens of His sincerity, the price that He paid that sinners might be saved in looking to Him. And will you and I be the ones to say, "I have nothing to say, nowhere to go, not a word to utter"?

Christ died for sinners, not just in Palestine, Rome, Corinth, Colosse, Galatia, or any other particular cities, towns, and places. Christ died for sinners not just in days past or in times of unusual divine activity or in the lives of the men and women whom history has marked out as worthy of attention. The issue is not whether we believe in the doctrine of election. We do not know who God's elect are until they believe. But the brokenhearted person who has been reconciled to his God and is being made holy by God's grace in Christ is not prepared to see Christ's honor laid low because he is too fearful to tell of the Jesus who loved him and gave Himself for him; he is not willing to miss opportunities to see sinners saved in his time and place, redeemed men and women who will bring honor and glory to Christ in his own generation.

Consider again what is at stake for those without Christ. Their very souls are on the line. They may hate to read such words as you will write and speak, and they might loathe the pleadings of parents and pastors, but do you not feel the weight of this undeniable obligation, and—out of love for souls—will you not go on speaking and pleading, over and over again? Why? Because though you may be hated, you love enough to go on speaking. You love enough to teach others God's ways. You see what it is to be lost and undone without Christ because you have felt the weight of sin. You therefore urge sinners to fly to Christ without delay: "Go as you are, go without any pride or self-reliance, go as a penitent sinner to the cross of the Lord Jesus, and there receive pardon for all your sins." You remind yourself, "If Jesus loved me and gave Himself for me, then I will and must—in loving Him—seek His glory by my efforts for the salvation of others." The preacher and hymn writer John Cennick felt this and expressed it poetically. Notice how he moves from the reality of salvation received to the urgency of salvation declared, and then pray that you might trace the same trajectory in your own heart and experience:

> Lo! glad I come; and thou, dear Lamb,
> Shall take me to thee as I am!
> Nothing but sin I thee can give;
> Yet help me, and thy praise I'll live!
>
> I'll tell to all poor sinners round
> What a dear Saviour I have found;
> I'll point to thy redeeming blood,
> And say, "Behold the Way to God!"[26]

The Glory of God

What is it to be an unsaved sinner? It is to be one who robs God of His glory. Every thought in the mind, word on the tongue, and deed in the flesh of an ungodly man or woman dishonors the God whom the Christian professes to love. There is no fear or adoration of or reverence for the God of our salvation (Ps. 36:1). God has done great things for us, and we are glad (Ps. 126:3); the nations are supposed to see it and declare that God *has* done great things for us (v. 2)! God is to be honored, glorified, and praised. But what is our God to the age in which we live? He is usually considered a mere figment of deluded imaginations. Are we prepared to see Almighty God discarded and despised in our generation? If we are, then we can walk away and keep our mouths shut. But can we accept the contempt, wickedness, and ungodliness of the ignorance and hatred of God that we see demonstrated all around us as reasonable and righteous without saying a single word in His honor? What is the glory of God to us? Are we the people of God? Has God

---

26. John Cennick, *Life and Hymns of John Cennick*, ed. J. R. Broome (Harpenden, England: Gospel Standard Trust Publications, 1988), hymn 154.

not, as it were, pinned His glory to us in this world (Dan. 9:19)? And are we willing to hold our tongues, shut our mouths, and speak not a word while our glorious triune God is trampled upon in the minds and hearts and lives of the men and women with and around whom we live?

There is a story told of a meeting during the nineteenth century. It was the time of the Downgrade Controversy, when a lack of faithfulness to the plain witness of Scripture was being intellectualized. An old woman went to hear a young disciple of the radical humanist and godless deist Thomas Paine,[27] and she heard this man as he disdainfully claimed to disprove the existence of God. As was the habit of the speaker, when he had finished, he asked if anyone had any questions. He had done this many times, and he thought he knew everything to expect. Up came that old woman, poor and twisted, and she stood on the platform and delivered her testimony of how her husband had died in her youth, leaving her with several children to care for and how she had cried out to Christ day after day. She had lived in constant dependence on God; she had looked to Him hour by hour, not just for her salvation but for every good thing that would follow after. God, she said, had always been pleased to feed and clothe her, to save her children from their sins, giving her strong and upright sons and godly young women as daughters. God was still sustaining her, feeding her soul through the Scriptures in her own private reading and by hearing them preached by a faithful man of God. She had tested God in all her trials and circumstances and knew Him to be true and good—she had proof! Though the boastful young man tried to mock her, she held her ground, so concerned that God's honor would not suffer while she had a mouth to open and a tongue to speak, that she stood up and exposed herself to the empty but painful ridicule of hundreds in order that Christ and His Father might not be trampled upon before men.

---

27. Thomas Paine (1737–1809) was a British radical, author, pamphleteer, propagandist, and revolutionary who unashamedly rejected biblical religion and embraced deism in his life and writings, elevating human reason above divine revelation as the guide to belief and behavior. He was very much a figurehead for the movement, acknowledged by supporters and answered by opponents as such.

How concerned are you for the glory of God in Jesus Christ? If you are a child of God, you have been plucked as a brand from the burning. You deserve hell, and you have been granted heaven. Your sins have been forgiven through the blood of God's own Son, Jesus Christ, whom He gave as the ransom price for you while you were still willingly consumed by your sin. And now you live to the praise of the glory of God. Nowhere is the power and wisdom of God more gloriously displayed than in the good news of Christ crucified, and there is nothing that the saved sinner desires more than the display of God's glory. We will no longer rob God of His glory in our own lives, and we long to promote it in the lives of others. This is David's next step in the tearful song of the brokenhearted evangelist, expressing fervent desires for the glory of God in the declaration of His righteousness from the broken and contrite heart of a repenting person:

> Deliver me from the guilt of bloodshed, O God,
>> The God of my salvation,
>> And my tongue shall sing aloud of Your righteousness.
> O Lord, open my lips,
>> And my mouth shall show forth Your praise.
> For You do not desire sacrifice, or else I would give it;
>> You do not delight in burnt offering.
> The sacrifices of God are a broken spirit,
>> A broken and a contrite heart—
>> These, O God, You will not despise.
> Do good in Your good pleasure to Zion;
>> Build the walls of Jerusalem.
> Then You shall be pleased with the sacrifices of righteousness,
>> With burnt offering and whole burnt offering;
>> Then they shall offer bulls on Your altar (Ps. 51:14–19).

So, brothers and sisters in Christ: What of you and me? Christian, this is an undeniable obligation. It is a simple question: Will you obey? You are enlisted in the army of the Lamb. Are you prepared to go forth as one of Christ's troops to do battle? You might have questions and concerns, and there is more detail, information, help, instruction, and comfort that we need, but—at root—do you have this desire? We might feel our weakness and wish to be better equipped—we might wish a thousand things—but here we are, and here is the task. Do you have this settled determination? Do you feel the weight of these things pressing in upon your soul? As a pardoned sinner you must make it your principled resolution that you will join David in the ranks of the brokenhearted evangelists, teaching God's ways to transgressors in order that sinners might be converted to Him and that the glory and honor of God in Jesus Christ shall not suffer while you have a part to play.

CHAPTER 2

AM I EFFECTIVE?
Our Necessary Equipment

We have an undeniable obligation to teach transgressors God's ways. Proclaiming Christ is the life business of the Christian. We must rightly and fairly recognize that some Christians are called to preach the good news as a matter of particular vocation, and others are not. At the same time, whether or not we make our living by the gospel (1 Cor. 9:14), proclaiming Jesus as Lord and Christ is an obligation upon every redeemed soul. The *sphere* of the work may be different, but its *nature* is the same. As one who had received pardon for his sins, David engaged in teaching transgressors God's ways as nothing more or less than a pardoned sinner. If we partake of that character, then we must also engage in this profoundly personal and humbling responsibility, a task in which so much is at stake—ultimately, the glory and honor of the triune God.

Some might feel overwhelmed, staggering under the weight of a felt obligation. Stunned by our own manifest weakness, we may wonder how anyone can begin to accomplish something of such magnitude: "It is too much, too high, too great. I am not sure that I can undertake it." The fear of man is an especially powerful snare, and we are often crippled by a desperate desire to avoid criticism or win applause. Others might feel charged up and enthusiastic: "Yes, this is something we must do, something *I* must do. I am ready to go home and speak to that person, to go into my place of work and begin to speak again for Jesus Christ." Perhaps, though, there follows closely after an accompanying sense of, "What will I say, and how will I do it, and what will happen, especially if it all falls flat?" There is a desire to labor but perhaps a degree of confusion as to the nature and undertaking of such labor. There may be other issues that are raised in your mind, other questions that you have: "How do I do this? Where do I start? What do I do? How do I keep going when it seems to be falling apart?"

Robert Candlish speaks quaintly but accurately of the doubts and fears we can feel:

> But how to set about the good work is what perplexes me. It seems so difficult and delicate an affair. There are so many considerations of prudence and propriety to be taken into account; so many snares into which I may fall, or mistakes which I may commit; so much risk of doing more harm than good;—I am so sensitively alive to the charge of ostentation and hypocrisy, or the appearance of hypocrisy, and see so clearly how worldly friends may be offended by injudicious zeal and the unreasonable intrusion of spiritual topics; I have such an impression of the sacredness of the ark of God, and such a shrinking dread of handling it, with the best intentions, unworthily or unwisely;—that I am rather disposed to keep silence, and leave it to more advanced Christians, experienced veterans, to vindicate God's ways, and rebuke men's sins, and win their souls![1]

Have you felt any of this? Are you conscious of how much could go wrong? Of the possibility that you might actually damage Christ's cause rather than advance it? Are you more aware of your sin than you are of God's grace and perhaps hindered in your declaration of His goodness? Do you see how quickly you could trample on toes and cause unnecessary offense? Are you conscious that you are dealing with holy things and fearful of somehow profaning the truth by mishandling them? Candlish goes on to warn us "how much guilt is contracted, how much evil is done, how much good left undone, how much sin suffered in a brother, how many souls allowed to go on in the broad way, through professing Christians, and even true believers, yielding to such timid reasoning."[2]

---

1. Candlish, *Prayer of a Broken Heart*, 78.
2. Candlish, *Prayer of a Broken Heart*, 79.

Let us not, then, yield to timid reasoning! In order, with God's help, to encourage the overwhelmed, instruct the eager, and direct the willing, we need first to consider our necessary equipment. If the first question we tried to answer was "Am I willing?" then the second question is "How can I be effective? What do I need to accomplish the task? How can I be a faithful and—God willing—fruitful evangelist?"

Someone might also challenge the idea that any equipment is actually necessary. Do we really *need* anything when God is sovereign? Can't God bless apart from, without, or even against certain means employed? Is God not able to accomplish whatever He pleases by whatever instrument He chooses? Doesn't God use bad people to accomplish good ends?

There is undoubted truth here. Elias Keach, son of the Calvinistic Baptist pastor Benjamin Keach, was actually converted while preaching a sermon to others, an occurrence rare but not unique. Perhaps the most famous instance of this in the United Kingdom was the experience of William Haslam, an Anglo-Catholic vicar in Cornwall during the nineteenth century. Coming by various means under a strong conviction of sin, he determined not to preach until he should have resolved the matter. However,

> the sun was shining brightly, and before I could make up my mind to put off the service, the bells struck out a merry peal, and sent their summons far away over the hills. Now the thought came to me that I would go to church and read the morning prayers and after that dismiss the people. There was no preparation for the Holy Communion that day, and I had deputed the clerk to select the hymns, for I was far too ill to attend to anything myself. The psalms and hymns were especially applicable to my case, and seemed to help me, so that I thought I would go on and read the ante-communion service, and then dismiss the people. And while I was reading the Gospel, I thought, well, I will just say a few words in explanation of this, and then I will dismiss them. So I went up into the pulpit and gave out my text. I took it from the gospel of the day—"What think ye of Christ?" (Matt. 22:42).
>
> As I went on to explain the passage, I saw that the Pharisees and scribes did not know that Christ was the Son of God, or that He was come to save them. They were looking for a king, the son

of David, to reign over them as they were. Something was telling me, all the time, "You are no better than the Pharisees yourself— you do not believe that He is the Son of God, and that He is come to save you, any more than they did." I do not remember all I said, but I felt a wonderful light and joy coming into my soul, and I was beginning to see what the Pharisees did not. Whether it was something in my words, or my manner, or my look, I know not; but all of a sudden a local preacher, who happened to be in the congregation, stood up, and putting up his arms, shouted out in a Cornish manner, "The parson is converted! The parson is converted! Hallelujah!" and in another moment his voice was lost in the shouts and praises of three or four hundred of the congregation. Instead of rebuking this extraordinary "brawling," as I should have done in a former time, I joined in the outburst of praise; and to make it more orderly, I gave out the Doxology— "Praise God, from whom all blessings flow"—and the people sang it with heart and voice, over and over again.[3]

While such occurrences may be exceedingly rare, we must not deny that God's power and wisdom are such as to enable Him to draw a straight line with a crooked stick.

Others are truly converted when Christ is preached from wrong motives or without genuine gospel clarity. Simply because the gospel is the Word of God and will accomplish that for which God has sent it (Isa. 55:11), it is possible that even without the things addressed here, God might still be pleased to make it fruitful in salvation. Grace has overcome, and continues to overcome, our constitutional sins and failings, so that we are productive in this task despite ourselves; the treasure is in earthen vessels in order that the excellence of the power may be of God and not of man (2 Cor. 4:7).

However, we are looking particularly at the personal and humbling labor of willingly witnessing to Jesus Christ with an eye to the glory of God in the salvation of men and women. If we are to be consistent in that endeavor, in our faithfulness to the work and our fruitfulness by that

---

3. William Haslam, *From Death into Life* (London: Morgan & Scott, n.d.), 60–61.

work, then certain things must be foundational in our labors and expectation of success. There is a real sense in which, for sustained and earnest endeavor and fruitfulness, we are likely to be crippled without those things we will consider (though we will not tie God's hands and limit the Holy One of Israel). As we have noted before, the first twelve verses of Psalm 51—all the pleas for pardon and all the prayers for grace—pour themselves into verse 13. However, the realities of verse 12 are those that particularly drive the activity of verse 13: "Restore to me the joy of Your salvation, and uphold me by Your generous Spirit. *Then* I will teach transgressors Your ways, and sinners shall be converted to You."

We must bring verse 12 into its legitimate contact with verse 13, seeing how the joy and blessing of verse 12 relate to our undeniable obligation to teach transgressors the way of God. We should note those things not in themselves essential before turning, positively, to our indispensable equipment, together with some practical counsels.

Things Not in Themselves Essential

Many things are not completely useless, but neither are they the foundation of genuine evangelistic success. We are often put off or even crippled in our labors for the extension of Christ's kingdom by doubts, fears, and uncertainties. We look to ourselves rather than to God, and we see in ourselves hundreds of reasons we will not be very effective. We look at what we are *not* and the task that lies ahead of us, and it is easy to become despondent and downcast and to think that the work is hopeless. Perhaps we are tempted to imagine that we need "something special" in order to be effective as a witness to Jesus Christ, some personal or theological or oratorical wizardry, something that sets us apart from the herd of "ordinary" Christians. We look to certain qualities or gifts and say, "Well, if only that were true of me, then I would be able to accomplish something." But, on the basis of what God says in Psalm 51, there are clearly several things that are *not* in themselves essential equipment for the work of evangelism. Some of these qualities and gifts certainly may be used of God to make someone particularly useful, but none is indispensably necessary for fruitfulness.

We Do Not Need a Special Calling

The only calling that we need in order to consider ourselves a witness to Christ is the call to follow Him. Simply being a Christian constitutes our calling for this work. Remember Matthew Henry's assertion: "Penitents should be preachers." It is not necessary that we be recognized, formal preachers of Jesus Christ in order to be witnesses to Jesus Christ. We do not require a badge or title that declares "Evangelist" to engage in this task. There is no need for us to be set apart in any particular congregation, by any special or extraordinary act, for this basic work of taking the gospel to the unconverted. No special dispensation is needed from the church or its officers to undertake this labor in the ordinary sense; no one need ask permission to witness to Christ in his or her appointed sphere. This is not to suggest that there are no particular callings and offices and functions requiring the recognition by Christ's church of Christ's gifts to His church. With respect to these there is a very real sense in which we must not run before we are sent by Christ and His disciples (Rom. 10:14–15). There are some particular expressions of this duty that may require the sanction and oversight of the appointed undershepherds of the church or the endorsement of the church as a whole, for the sake of Christ's honor and in recognition of church order. However, once all that is taken into account, it remains true that this is a privilege and an obligation from which no healthy and obedient saint is excluded. Archibald Alexander puts it forcefully:

> The greatest charity in the world is the communication of divine truth to the ignorant. Must all preach the word? Yes, in a certain sense, and according to their ability, and in observance of due order. All may teach. All Christians are bound to teach—the parent his children, the master his servants, the schoolmaster his scholars, the citizen his more ignorant neighbours, the colporteur [carrier of books and other literature] the families he visits with books and tracts, the pastor his flock, and the missionary the unconverted Jew and heathen. Here is work enough for all, and all may labor in their appropriate sphere; but all

must labor: the duty is incumbent on them, and the obligation cannot be evaded.[4]

We expect no further ordinary direction or any extraordinary direction from heaven to tell us to go. We already have all we need to send us into the path of witness to Jesus Christ.

We Do Not Need a Piercing Intellect

We must be careful here, as we are not suggesting that one can simply spout inaccurate and untruthful nonsense and still be an effective evangelist, and this is a matter we will consider later. Nevertheless, we can be sure that effective evangelism is not necessarily bound up with mere academic qualifications or intellectual attainments. No one requires an IQ of genius level or a piece of paper that labels us a master of theology or doctor of divinity in order to speak of Christ. There is no required reading of a list of theological tomes, no examination to pass. There is no requirement to study in a concentrated fashion for a set number of hours before being let loose. Too often, perhaps, we think we need to understand all the mysteries contained in Scripture before we can speak, when even Peter acknowledged that there were some things hard to understand. We might imagine that unless we have reached the level at which we can explain everything there is no point in opening our mouths. But there is no need to attain to a high academic standard in any discipline in order to be a useful tool in the hand of God in testifying of Jesus Christ. There are some things that it would most certainly be profitable to possess, and sanctified intelligence can be a great benefit, but no one is disqualified through the absence of intellectual ability and academic qualifications.

We Do Not Need Worldly Eloquence

Ready speech does not equip us by its presence or prevent us by its absence. A good talker is not necessarily a good evangelist, and sometimes quite the opposite. "The gift of the gab" can prevent a person from

---

4. Alexander, *Practical Truths*, 34.

being a profitable servant of Christ in this regard because some can only talk and have never learned to listen. You might be tempted to think that the ability to spin out a conversation with long words and ornate phrases is desirable, but that often does more harm than good. Such wordy nonsense often serves only to confuse those with whom we are speaking. They would do better with the good, plain speech that J. C. Ryle recommends: "Unless you are simple…you will never be understood, and unless you are understood you cannot do good to those who hear you."[5] Wordiness should not be mistaken for genuine eloquence, which springs more from the heart than from the lips. To be effective in soul-winning we do not need to be able to tickle people's ears or be able to stand up and command a crowd of people with the power of our words. True eloquence is not the power to set off verbal fireworks on demand.

We Do Not Need a Disposable Income

Wealth will not entitle us to a true hearing for the gospel. We might wish for added opportunities to do good to people's bodies, and that might open a door to their hearts, but while you might be able briefly to buy a person's ear, you certainly cannot buy his soul. Nothing that is possessed in this life upon earth is, in and of itself, essential to evangelistic success.

We Do Not Need Intensive Training

We might wish for some kind of training, but some of the most truly successful evangelists have been untrained men. Consider Billy Bray, a foul-mouthed and licentious tin miner from Cornwall, converted by the power of God. He was an unorthodox man who would dance down the streets singing "Glory!" so taken up was he with the realities of the salvation he had obtained in Jesus Christ. Untrained, Bray began to exhort people to follow his Christ and saw much of God's blessing upon his labors. We do not by any means despise learning. Indeed,

---

5. J. C. Ryle, "Simplicity in Preaching," in *The Upper Room: Being a Few Truths for the Times* (Edinburgh: Banner of Truth, 1970), 36. His whole essay is worth reading in this regard.

every Christian should pursue a deep and accurate understanding of the truth of God, using whatever legitimate means are available. We can and should seek to advance in our ability to communicate the truth concerning Christ Jesus, and we can receive instruction and direction in this. However, we need no qualification as an evangelist, no school or college, and no set period of learning before we begin to speak for Jesus Christ. No training in and of itself will guarantee our effectiveness in the task of witness.

We Do Not Need a Particular Character or Temperament

"If I were only a little more like such-and-such a person," says one. Or we hear, "So-and-so has the right personality for the work of evangelism: he's very outgoing, but I am not.... That lady finds it easy to speak to people, but I don't.... That other guy finds it easy to begin conversations, but I stutter and stumble." Read your way through the New Testament and consider at the very least the character of the twelve apostles as outlined in the gospel histories and letters. Consider the character and gifts of Paul, Peter, John, and other men whose personalities decorate the pages of the Scripture that they were inspired to write. Think of Isaiah, Jeremiah, or Ezekiel. How different these men were from one another: their calls were different, yet each was humbled before God. Their characters were different, their constitutions were different, and so they were employed to carry messages with a different tone or emphasis. Robert Murray M'Cheyne writes, "I oft read with pleasure to soothe or engage, Isaiah's wild measure or John's simple page."[6] What does he mean? Admittedly speaking of a time when he read the Scriptures as a literary work in which to take natural pleasure rather than as a message of life to save his soul, he nevertheless recognizes different characters crafting different sentences under the influences of God's Spirit—the rough rhythms of Isaiah's poetry or the clear but profound declarations of John—each one blessed by God as

---

6. Robert Murray M'Cheyne, "Jehovah Tsidkenu," in *Memoir and Remains of Robert Murray M'Cheyne* by Andrew A. Bonar (1892; repr., London: Banner of Truth, 1966), 632–33.

he undertook his particular sphere of labor in the character and with the personality God had bestowed on him. Paul himself said, "By the grace of God I am what I am" (1 Cor. 15:10). He had no desire to alter his fundamental character, because grace does not war against nature but rather renews and redeems it. What we are before conversion we will be after conversion, but made new, energized with new motives and driven by a new power. We will be purified and animated, enabled to lay our gifts and graces upon the altar as a sacrifice to Jesus Christ. Some are ebullient and outgoing and will remain so, tempered by grace. Some are fiery and will be grace-softened without losing their vigor. Others are more phlegmatic or meditative and will continue to be so, but stirred by spiritual realities. We know extroverts and introverts, those who tend toward melancholy or enthusiasm, but all need to be sanctified by the grace of God in Christ, and no one character type qualifies or disqualifies us; no one can shrug off these responsibilities.

All of these particular things, and a host of others, may—in certain times, places, circumstances, and ways—have an impact on gospel success, under God. You think of someone like Spurgeon: he was called to be a minister of the gospel, had a piercing intellect, and possessed a powerful natural eloquence. He did not have a great disposable income when he began the work, and what money came to him in the course of his gospel success was quickly distributed with gospel motives and aims. He had no formal training, and his particular character defies simple description. But he was a man who saw much blessing by God upon his labors in the name of Christ. All that he was, in its right role within the whole man, was used by God for the salvation of sinners. Put up a thousand men alongside Spurgeon; put yourself alongside him. You must acknowledge that any or all of those gifts and graces probably would, if we had them, be profitable in some way. However, we must likewise acknowledge that none of them—in and of themselves, nor all of them taken together—is absolutely essential for us if we are to go out and undertake the work of testifying to Jesus Christ. All of them, without a broken heart, will lie fallow.

In other words, the absence of any of these things is, in and of itself, no cause for delay. You cannot wait until you have them all before you start this work. None of them, in their presence or absence, is any cause for boasting or despair, as they are not in themselves essential to gospel success. None of them, singly or in any combination, is an excuse for you or me to avoid the work of teaching transgressors God's ways. Witnessing is our undeniable obligation whether we have some, all, or none of those qualities or gifts outlined above. Consider the growth of the early church: there are several occasions in which there are no "big names" or "big gifts" associated with the rapid and effectual spread of gospel truth. In Acts 11:19–21, we read of ordinary Christians scattered after the persecution that arose over Stephen. These men and women traveled in a variety of directions, and as they went they "preached the Word" or preached "the Lord Jesus." No miracles are recorded as attending this ministry, no apostles or their immediate companions are mentioned, no unusual means are employed, but because "the hand of the Lord was with them…a great number believed and turned to the Lord." Like these brothers, we have no need to wait, neither have we any cause for despondency, and still less do we have any excuse to remain silent.

Our Necessary Equipment

If those things are not in themselves essential, what is? What is indispensable for the permanent, consistent, fruitful, ongoing labor of evangelism? There are two things suggested here in Psalm 51:12: the joy of God's salvation and a life of consistent godliness.

The Joy of God's Salvation

Matthew Poole defines the joy of God's salvation as "the comfortable sense of [His] saving grace and help, promised and vouchsafed to me, both for my present and everlasting salvation."[7] That is a brief but sweetly accurate definition. What Poole is describing, and what David is crying out for, is the felt reality of divine truth—the joy of God's salvation, or gratitude for grace received. He speaks of the comforts of real religion, the sense that I am God's and He is mine and that nothing can

---

7. Matthew Poole, *Psalms–Malachi*, vol. 2 of *A Commentary on the Holy Bible* (Edinburgh: Banner of Truth, 1962), 84.

or ever will come between us. This is the present experience of God's smile upon him, His ready grace and help, a sense of the truth of the promises of God, a knowing and feeling that God is his now and forevermore. It is not just a public demonstration of the comforts of true religion, but it is the private presence and reality of them. This man knows that even if he is isolated from all other blessing, God is his portion; whether alone or in the presence of other men, he knows that he is God's. When God works these realities out in David's life—when he sees, knows, and feels them as one in happy communion with God—he experiences the joy of God's salvation.

But what if we do not have any present sense of this joy ourselves? To be sure, the first necessity is that we be saved, blessed in the new covenant in Christ Jesus. At the same time, we must remember that the absence of this joy is not necessarily the same as the absence of salvation. The cry to God to make His face shine upon us is often the cry of His people lamenting His felt distance from them. Indeed, it is more than possible—in many senses it is entirely healthy—to be persuaded that we are children of God, and yet to long for more of God's presence with us. We want a joy of the right kind (not just an emotional buzz or the mere froth of carnal excitement, but a deeply rooted delight in salvation by Christ) and of growing degree (drawing nearer to God in Christ as our sense of these things advances).

So how does a child of God pursue the increasing joy of a possessed salvation? There is no better place to start than the beginning. The best place is the cross of Jesus Christ. If we would have our hearts stirred by redemption realities, then we must walk again in Gethsemane where He is weeping and at Gabbatha where He is tried and upon Golgotha where He is crucified, and we must dwell upon what is taking place as Jesus, the incarnate Son of God, suffers and dies for His people. We must walk in the early morning in the garden with the freshly empty tomb. We must stand gazing into heaven, conscious that this same Jesus ever lives to intercede for His redeemed and will come again as He once went, but apart from sin for salvation. Iain Murray gives the following counsel:

Supposing we had lived in Puritan times and we went to our pastor with the regret that while we believed in God's love it did not move us very much. If the pastor had reason to think that the complaint was being expressed by a genuine Christian it is certain that one of the first questions we would face is this, "How regularly are you spending time meditating on what you say you believe?" Their judgement was that hearing sermons, even reading the Bible, will do little good if that is where we stop. "Meditation," says Brooks, "is the food of your souls, it is the very stomach and natural heat whereby spiritual truths are digested. A man shall as soon live without his heart, as he shall be able to get good by what he reads without meditation.... They usually thrive best who meditate most. Meditation is a soul-fattening duty; it is a grace-strengthening duty; it is a duty-crowning duty."[8]

Concerning the love of God, Murray then quotes John Downame's *Guide to Godlyness*: "'Now the means whereby our hearts may be inflamed with this divine fire of God's love, are, first, that we often meditate upon God's infinite goodness, excellency, beauty, and perfection, which make him worthy of all love, and how he has exercised these saving attributes towards us...giving his only Son to die for us.'"[9]

If we would have holy emotions genuinely stirred up—a freshly accurate sense of sin, a more profound awareness of forgiveness, a deeper grasp on the love of God toward sinful men, with a corresponding joy in God's grace in Christ—then we must meditate upon those central truths of God's character revealed in the being and doing of His Son, the Lord Christ. Then we might anticipate that our joy will increase.

The register of this joy is not necessarily a smile upon a man's face or a tear trickling down his cheek or even the antics of a Billy Bray, dancing down the street and shouting "Glory!" Bray once said that if you tried to shut him up in a barrel, he would shout "Glory!" out through

---

8. Iain H. Murray, "The Puritans on Maintaining Spiritual Zeal," in *Adorning the Doctrine: Papers Read at the 1995 Westminster Conference* (London: Westminster Conference, 1995), 87.

9. Murray, "Puritans on Maintaining Spiritual Zeal," 88.

the bunghole.[10] However, others are naturally more melancholy or less extroverted in their disposition; under the unfortunate circumstance of being shut into a barrel, their response might reasonably be different to that of Billy Bray. A story is told of two Scotsmen, one of whom observed his lighthearted and witty young colleague joking and enjoying his time among a family they were visiting. The young man was then asked to pray, and he knelt down. Out of his mouth came a stream of holy eloquence as he pleaded earnestly and joyfully for the souls of the unconverted and for God's richest blessing upon them all. The older man said to his younger colleague that if he had played like him, it would have been some days altogether before he could have prayed like him. Why? Because they had distinctly different characters, and the manifestation of the joy of God's salvation was to some extent according to that character, though it might have been equal in degree. Both could sing aloud of God's righteousness with a mouth showing forth God's praise (Ps. 51:14–15), though one might sing in a minor and the other in a major key. We have, perhaps, smiled at the preacher who with a face as long as a month of Mondays assures the congregation of his profound delight at being granted the privilege of ministering God's Word in such pleasant company. Others could not begin to express the same sincerely felt affection without it playing across their smiling faces.

But these various men, though so different in so many ways, had a sense of the reality of God's truth. They knew what it was to be saved by grace. They were not merely in the first flush of the realities of salvation. Their pleasure and joy were not governed by circumstance, nor were they the result of temperament. This conviction is a result of knowing that God is. It is a result of knowing that the God who is, is the God of Scripture. It is a result of knowing that the God of Scripture is our God and has a hold upon our souls with an unshakeable grip, a grip that then liberates them and us to be the men or women God would have us be. Such men are examples of those who knew rest and peace, who learned of Christ. These are men who wore the yoke, who were bearing

---

10. John Tallach, *God Made Them Great* (Edinburgh: Banner of Truth, 1975), 67.

the light burden of the service of Jesus Christ and who therefore had rest in their souls, because they were walking, to an increasing extent, in step with Christ by His Spirit. It was the peace of holiness pursued, the joy of a close relationship with God in the fear of the Lord, the reality of communion with the most high and triune God, and the known and felt sense of all the comforts of true religion in degree, if not in totality. The joy of God's salvation is the stable peace, the "solid joys and lasting treasure,"[11] of a faithful bondslave of Jesus Christ.

These things give us good matter to speak to the unconverted. What do you have to tell them? You can speak of your experience. Even if you know nothing more than this, you know that God has saved you from your sins, that Christ has been your Savior. You know what it is to come from darkness to light; you know what it is to be dead but now to live. You can tell them—if you can tell them nothing else—what Christ is to you. And it will give you not just good matter, but it will give you a good manner, because you will speak out of sympathy for the lost. You know from your own experience what it is to grieve over sin and what it is to receive the lovingkindnesses of a merciful God.

With such experience you will never put yourself on a pedestal. Rather, you should display the meekness and lowliness that suit a servant of Christ, coming to others as you really are when everything else is stripped away: a sinner saved by the grace of God. You must come without pretension, without drawing attention to yourself, saying, in effect, "I am like you, but for grace. I was just what you are and where you are, and would be still, but God has saved me. There is nothing in me that lifts me above you or any other creature of God but the mercy and grace of God in Jesus Christ." Bunyan said of his preaching, "I preached what I felt, what I smartingly did feel."[12] That is true eloquence: not high-sounding words or long, convoluted sentences, but to feel what you speak and to speak what you most penetratingly do feel. But when the joy of God's salvation is a present reality in your heart and soul, you will speak what you feel, and you will speak with a burning eloquence

---

11. John Newton, "Glorious Things of Thee Are Spoken," stanza 5.
12. Bunyan, *Grace Abounding*, 70.

that no one can stop. The apostles declared to the Sanhedrin, "We cannot but speak the things which we have seen and heard" (Acts 4:20).

Some might say, "But I do not feel the joy of my salvation as I wish I did! How can I speak it?" Speak what you have with courage and confidence in Christ, and it may be that this will prove the very means of stirring up increased joy. Remember Spurgeon: "I believe that the not seeking to win souls brings many spiritual maladies upon Christian men.... God in discipline often brings sorrow upon his own people because of their unholy silence as to gracious things."[13] He then offers a cheerfully selfish reason why we should go about the business of soul winning, realistic and yet encouraging:

> Who does not like to be the bearer of good news? The pleasant tale of redeeming grace and dying love, the pleasant story of a Saviour who came from heaven to earth, to lift us up from earth to heaven, the story of our own conversion, the story of God's goodness since our conversion—why, it must be delightful to tell it! And when you have spoken for Jesus, if you succeed in converting a sinner to God, then comes the pleasure! Great is the mother's joy when she looks upon her firstborn child. She remembers no more her travail for joy that a man is born into the world! I am sure, however, that the pleasure is greater of looking upon a newborn child of God, and remembering no more your anguish over that soul, and your care in seeking to bring it to Jesus, because you have such bliss in knowing that there is one soul the more to decorate the Redeemer's crown! Happy are our lives who can win souls! *I am very apt to be cast down and distressed in soul; but, next to fellowship with my Lord, my greatest consolation is found in receiving glad tidings of souls saved.* Here comes a letter of loving thanks from Ceylon, and another from the north of Norway, saying, "Blessed be God that I read your sermons and found a Saviour." From America I hear of an eminent Jewish Rabbi who has become a Baptist minister through reading one of my discourses, and anon I receive a letter from Havannah from a sailor who had just left the hospital, and tells me how the man who died

13. Spurgeon, "Christian's Great Business," 499.

in the next bed told him that he had a treasure which he would give him if he would take care of it, and he then handed him a number of my sermons stitched together. "They have saved my soul," he said, "and I hope they will save yours." The sailor who writes blesses God in a warm-hearted way that it is so and the sermons have led him to Jesus. Is this not joy? Would you not like to share it?"[14]

Let us be honest: most of us are not going to receive floods of soul-warming letters from the four corners of the globe testifying to our usefulness in God's kingdom, but those of us who have had even one e-mail or note from a friend letting us know that God used our feeble, stumbling words—used them, perhaps, when we were ourselves struggling against ungodliness or wrestling with melancholy—to bring a soul to Jesus can testify to the profound joy in God's salvation that is stirred up.

When we have the joy of God's salvation we speak *as angels cannot speak*. They have no experience of the saving grace of Christ as do redeemed sinners. Angels know what it is to be kept by the power of Christ, but they cannot speak of the joys of being saved through the blood of Jesus Christ. They might be able to build a golden boat of truth, compared with our wooden vessel, because they are sinless spirits, and they can speak in a way that we cannot match. But our boat is borne on the current of redeeming love, carried along by the stream of our experience of the grace of God, and it travels further and faster than the golden craft of angels.

We speak *as the devil will not speak*. He knows what it is to sin, what it is to fall to the lowest point, but he has no experience of salvation, and he hates the truth and will never point a person to Christ, except as an object of ridicule or hatred. He knows God with an intellectual accuracy that might beggar the learning of great theologians, but there is no desire for or love to Him, no willingness that the God he knows as an almighty enemy might be known by humans as an almighty friend.

14. Spurgeon, "Christian's Great Business," 500, emphasis added.

We speak *as fallen men and women do not speak*. The truths concerning our Savior are truths spiritually discerned, and a person can be the greatest scholar in the entire world—even the greatest Bible scholar who ever walked the face of the earth—and yet not grasp the truth savingly. Without grace he has nothing to say. Erasmus, one of the greatest Greek scholars of the Renaissance, was the first man to put together the New Testament in Greek for a more modern audience, and yet, as time went on, it looked more and more as if Erasmus had never truly tasted the grace of God. No one had a mind like Erasmus. No one up to then might have entered into the intricacies of Greek quite as well as he, but he did not know from his heart what it was that he studied. So it was that when it came to the crunch, Erasmus really had nothing to offer to sinful and needy souls. You will get no fire from a dead man's belly. But to us who have tasted and seen that the Lord is good is committed a great responsibility and glorious opportunity to speak things that this world will never hear unless they come from our lips.

Remember that this is not a matter of calling, intellect, eloquence, training, or character. It is a matter of the broken heart now being bound up, and—with the joy of salvation again beginning to characterize the life of the penitent Christian—the truth of God's gracious dealings spilling over into the lives of those around us.

A Life of Consistent Godliness

The second part of our indispensable equipment requires that we pack into verse 12 what has already been said in verses 10 and 11:

> Create in me a clean heart, O God,
> And renew a steadfast spirit within me.
> Do not cast me away from Your presence,
> And do not take Your Holy Spirit from me.
> Restore to me the joy of Your salvation,
> And uphold me with Your generous Spirit.

How can we summarize these things? This is the godly life that is begun, established, and maintained by vital communion with God through Christ by the Holy Spirit. This is why David cries out, "Uphold me with Your generous Spirit." This is why he desires a clean heart within him and a steadfast spirit—no longer carried back and forth with every wind of doctrine, no longer falling prey to every temptation, no longer pulled this way or that by every so-called friend or word or exposure to some sin or pressure—but a heart that is fixed. Therefore he pleads with God that he might be upheld by God's generous Spirit. This is a man who, with his moral compass swinging round and holding to spiritual north, desires holiness above all other things and pursues it with all his heart and mind and soul and strength, in utter dependence upon the Spirit of God. This man wants to be as free from sin in his deeds as in his record, which has been blotted clean from all trace of iniquity. He wants in his heart and life the mirror image of the book of his sins washed clean by the blood of the heavenly Lamb. He desires to do, be, think, speak, and feel only in accordance with what God would have him do, be, think, speak, and feel.

This is the evident reality of grace in operation in the life of a redeemed sinner, by means of which he desires, pursues, and increasingly attains to genuine godliness. It is *evident reality*, not manifest absence or manifest perfection. On the one hand, then, it is not the life of a man wallowing in his sin. It is not the life of a woman sunk in angry despair over sin, living without God and hope in the world. It is not the life of someone who coasts along without regard to growth in grace and advance in holiness. But neither is it the person—who in truth does not exist—who has conquered every lust and overcome every enemy, who hurdles every barrier and bypasses every struggle. That would be the counsel of despair: "Only when you are a gleaming paragon of virtue may you dare to speak about Jesus." Which of us would ever open our mouths if this were the standard?

Rather, this is the life of a person at war with sin, his heart upheld by the Spirit of God as he seeks day by day to put sin to death in his thoughts, words, and deeds. It is a life of grace in which Jesus has, by His Spirit, taken up residence in the believer's heart (Eph. 3:16–17). Don Carson uses the analogy of a young couple scraping together enough money to buy a house in need of much investment of time and energy. He goes to work describing the ugly insufficiency of the premises, but then skips to the future:

The black and silver wallpaper has been replaced with tasteful pastel patterns. The couple has remodeled their kitchen, doing much of the work themselves. The roof no longer leaks, and the furnace has been replaced with a more powerful unit that also includes a central air conditioner. Better yet, as the family grows, this couple completes a couple of extra rooms in the basement and adds a small wing to serve as a study and sewing room. The grounds are neatly trimmed and boast a dazzling rock garden. Twenty-five years after the purchase, the husband one day remarks to his wife, "You know, I really like it here. This place suits us. Everywhere we look we see the results of our own labor. This house has been shaped to our needs and taste, and I really feel comfortable." When Christ by his Spirit takes up residence within us, he finds the moral equivalent of mounds of trash, black and silver wallpaper, and a leaking roof. He sets about turning this residence into a place appropriate for him, a place in which he is comfortable. There will be lots of cleaning to do, quite a few repairs, and some much-needed expansion. But his aim is clear: he wants to take up residence in our hearts, as we exercise faith in him.[15]

Now, middle-class idylls may not exactly float your boat—pastel patterns may not be your cup of tea, a sewing room in the new wing may not be the height of your ambition, and a rock garden may be anathema to you—but the point is clear: Jesus goes to work to renovate the reborn person's soul in order to make it a suitable dwelling place for Himself.

It is the process by which a believer works out his own salvation in fear and trembling for the very reason that God is at work in him to will and to do for His good pleasure (Phil. 2:12–13) that must be evident in a life, a process that begins with regeneration but is not over until glory dawns. It is a life in which progress is made, though often slowly. It is a life in which grace is powerfully operating, as sin is exposed, repented of, and addressed, sometimes slain with a thousand stabs over decades of attritional warfare. It shows itself in growing humility,

---

15. D. A. Carson, *A Call to Spiritual Reformation: Priorities from Paul and His Prayers* (Grand Rapids: Baker/IVP, 1992), 186.

in that gracious dynamic of holiness pursued, stumbling apparent, repentance expressed, forgiveness sought, faith exercised, and holiness pursued again. The brokenhearted evangelist is not a person proud of his perfection but rather confident in his God, not a person who thinks he has attained or is already perfected, but one who presses on that he may lay hold of that for which Christ Jesus has also laid hold on him (Phil. 3:12).

What are the effects of that consistent life of godliness pursued in dependence upon the Spirit of God? *Toward men*, it gives a testimony to the truth. It demonstrates the reality of our doctrine and shows that we live in accordance with what we say. It demonstrates the seriousness of what we speak—that when we talk about the need to be redeemed from sin and death and hell and the need to be free from iniquity, those are matters of the utmost seriousness. It demonstrates the fruit of faith, that there is a real putting off of sinful words and deeds with a genuine putting on of Christlike holiness that takes place, a process that renovates the human life. It is a lifestyle that wins a hearing for the gospel, because it unstops people's ears. It is a life that vindicates the gospel and the people of God from all charges of hypocrisy, because it presents a watertight case. It is the life that testifies to the conscience of the ungodly, because they see in it spiritual realities, things that they do not have and cannot have outside of Jesus Christ. It ministers to the need of those who are in need. It is a life that gives itself out in humble, self-denying obedience to Christ, putting others first. It is a life that maintains the honor of Christ, because you wear the badge of Christ while you name the name of Christ. It is a life that breaks—eventually—through many obstacles to love, a life that credibly displays the grace of God in Jesus Christ. It is an undeniable testimony to the reality of the truth we profess and teach.

It also has an effect *toward God*, because the blessing of God upon our labors is bound up with the pursuit and attainment of holiness. In a letter to a friend, the bright-hearted preacher Robert Murray M'Cheyne issued a clear reminder:

> Do not forget the culture of the inner man,—I mean of the heart.
> How diligently the cavalry officer keeps his sabre clean and

sharp; every stain he rubs off with the greatest care. Remember you are God's sword,—His instrument,—I trust a chosen vessel unto Him to bear His name. In great measure, according to the purity and perfection of the instrument, will be the success. It is not great talents God blesses so much as likeness to Jesus. A holy minister is an awful weapon in the hand of God.[16]

A close walk with God brings His people true and genuine fruitfulness. We need to pursue obedience to our God. We must be very quick to repent of any known sin, to cultivate a sensitive conscience that is always ready to be directed back to the Word and, by the Word, into paths of righteousness and peace. A close walk with God requires the pursuit of a way of living that does not grieve the Spirit of God. That is what David cries out to have. He has sinned, and sinned awfully, grieving the Spirit of God. He now confesses that without that Spirit upholding, sustaining, directing, governing, and enabling him to live a life of increasing godliness, he cannot begin to teach transgressors God's ways, because what he says would clash with what he is in himself.

Do we feel wretched failures at times? Do we return like a dog to its vomit, running back to sins we thought and hoped had long been overcome? Do vile thoughts, wicked words, and cruel deeds still spill out of us? Yes, and the brokenhearted evangelist mourns over such evidence of his sinful heart before God and men, but he demonstrates the vibrant realities of grace by going again to the fountain opened for sin and for uncleanness and by renewing his vows of willing obedience at the foot of the cross. It is hypocrisy to make grace a mere shelter for sin. It is reality to take our sins daily, even hourly, to the cross of Jesus and nail them there with Him and walk away with our consciences cleansed, our joy restored, and our duty clear. Such a person can and should speak of his Savior. He has a story of grace to tell!

And so David expresses his desire to speak, but he can only speak insofar as the Spirit of God upholds, enables, and equips him. And

16. Robert Murray M'Cheyne to the Rev. Dan Edwards, in *Memoir and Remains of Robert Murray M'Cheyne* by Andrew Bonar (Edinburgh: Banner of Truth, 1966), 282.

this is not a matter of wages, as if we undertake to be just so obedient in order that God will grant us just so many souls. It is a matter of promised blessing. There in the wilderness, with an entire nation before them knock-kneed and trembling because of the giants in the land that the Lord has given to them, Joshua and Caleb stand before thousands ready to turn and flee, and say: "If the LORD delights in us, then He will bring us into this land and give it to us, 'a land which flows with milk and honey.' Only do not rebel against the LORD, nor fear the people of the land, for they are our bread; their protection has departed from them, and the LORD is with us. Do not fear them" (Num. 14:8–9). "If the LORD delights in us…" What does the Lord delight in? He knows our frame and remembers that we are dust, but He has also saved us to be conformed to the image of His Son, and faith not only receives the imputed righteousness of Christ but is also the means whereby the imparted likeness of Jesus is more and more clearly seen in us. Likeness to Jesus delights God. Holiness delights God. The sincere obedience of His redeemed children delights God.

You see something similar at the beginning of the book of Psalms, in that declaration and testimony that hangs over the whole book:

> Blessed is the man
>> Who walks not in the counsel of the ungodly,
>> Nor stands in the path of sinners,
>> Nor sits in the seat of the scornful;
> But his delight is in the law of the LORD,
>> And in His law he meditates day and night (Ps. 1:1–2).

What shall happen to such a man?

> He shall be like a tree
>> Planted by the rivers of water,
>> That brings forth its fruit in its season,
>> Whose leaf also shall not wither;
> And whatever he does shall prosper (Ps. 1:3).

Do you see the connection? It is not the connection of wages earned—"I'll do this, and you give me that"—but rather a testimony that you and I should live in this way, and as we do so, God testifies that He will be pleased to smile upon our endeavors for His glory's sake. To live anything other than a life of consistent godliness in dependence upon the Spirit of God, especially in the matter of evangelism, is to thumb the nose at the God without whom we can do nothing. Of ourselves, we can do *nothing*! God can take away all our faculties in an instant if He so chooses. God can stop up our mouths, take away our ability to move, shut our eyes and ears, and render what we do utterly and completely worthless. God *knows* the way we live. It is not a matter of consistent performance and appearance before others; it is a matter of consistent and diligent holiness pursued before God. This is the God who declares that He desires truth in the hidden parts (Ps. 51:6). God's eyes scour our souls, and He says that His blessing rests upon obedience. If we therefore scorn that connection, refusing or ignoring the requirements for a consistent life of godliness in dependence upon the Spirit of God, who are we to expect that God would bless our best, let alone our worst, efforts to spread the gospel of Jesus Christ?

Why are these things our necessary equipment? Because they come from God. If there is no salvation outside the work of the Spirit of God—no power to open blind eyes; to unstop deaf ears; to soften hard hearts; to bring the glory of Christ evidently before the eyes of sinful people; to show those in need that their need is met in Jesus Christ; to reveal, to illuminate, and then to apply the blood of Christ in regenerating power; and to work the twin graces of faith and repentance in the souls of people previously ungodly—if no conversion takes place outside or beyond the work of God's Holy Spirit, then it is utterly indispensable that we do not grieve the very One upon whom the joy of our salvation and the consistent life of godliness depend, when those things are the very foundation upon which our testimony to fallen people is built. When a Christian rejoices in grace, being upheld by the Spirit of the Almighty in his pursuit of godliness, he has a gospel foundation for brokenhearted evangelism.

Some Practical Counsels

How should we assess ourselves in light of these things? What should be our response to the challenge of the obligation we feel and the equip-ment we need?

What Are You Waiting For?

What else is going to happen that has not already happened in order that we might engage in this Christian's life business of teaching trans-gressors God's ways? Have you and I been crippled by a false persuasion that we need something extra before we begin this work? I am not talking about the longing that we might have something more. If we are honest, I think we would all say that we sometimes wish we were a thousand times more than we are, and then we might just begin to feel ready to begin. But that feeling is not accurate, because Christ has already given all that we need for a life of fruitful godliness. If we are not speaking to sinners now, then it is very unlikely that a mere change of circumstance will lead to us speaking for Jesus. You might suddenly be constituted a great man or woman, given the most piercing and high of intellects, granted the capacity to speak with an eloquence that would put an angel to shame, given all the wealth that the world has to offer, sent on a stirring course of instruction in biblical means of evangelism, and had bestowed upon you a breadth of character suited to bringing the gospel to anyone alive upon the face of the earth. You could have all of those things, but unless you are ready to do the work now, however imperfectly, I wonder if you will ever begin to do the work. Too often we are ready to offer excuses:

- "Well, when things change a little bit, then I'll begin."

- "This is not the right environment; this is not the right place; these are not the right circumstances."

- "I'll wait until the gospel door is open a little wider, and then I will begin to speak."

- "I'll wait until they notice something different about me and ask me about it."

- "I'll wait until I have an opportunity that won't have any impact on my career."
- "I'll wait until I have an opportunity with someone where I am not worried about the fallout for the relationship."
- "I'll wait until there are no risks."

Do things ever change enough? Do you ever see one of those gaping opportunities when a sinner strides into view with a big sign on his head saying, "I'm the next in line of God's elect: hit me here now and the bells will ring"? It simply does not happen. Unless we begin now with what we have and are, in dependence upon the grace of God, we are unlikely to begin at all. Candlish presses us into action:

> Then open ye your own lips; at once; now; this very day. Wait not for any sign, or any impulse; any favourable opportunity; any pressing call. Begin now. Let some friend, or neighbour, hear you, ere the sun goes down, speaking a word in season; a word of admonition; a word of comfort; telling something of what the Lord is doing for your soul, and of his willingness to do the same for theirs. I call upon you thus to prove the earnestness of your repentance, and the strength of your resolution.[17]

What are we waiting for? We must improve what we have—yes! We must seek to be more and more the men and women that God would have us to be—yes! We must pursue prayerfully the joy of God's salvation and a consistent life of godliness—yes! But are we opening our mouths and teaching transgressors God's ways? Because if we are not now, nothing is likely to change that reality.

The Pursuit of Godliness

Are you earnestly seeking—by faith in Christ, through prayer, study, sitting under a sound and prayerful ministry of God's Word, and the pursuit of principled obedience—that inward and outward life of increasing godliness that is the true foundation of all fruitful witness? God has ordained certain means for the gathering in of His elect, but

---

17. Candlish, *Prayer of a Broken Heart*, 85–86.

this is the preparation to use those means. Imagine that you were circling on a space station high above the earth, and a problem became apparent with part of the machinery. You head over to see what is being done, and there is a man standing near the airlock with a box of tools, and he says, "I am going out to do the work. I have all the tools that are necessary in order to accomplish the task." Noticing a certain something missing, you take the trouble to remind him that he cannot go out until he has put on his spacesuit. He may have the tools he needs, but he cannot handle the environment he will be working in. He needs to be properly equipped in order to labor in that environment. The best tools available will not help you if you are not in yourself equipped to use those tools in the environment into which you must go. Thus it is with the Christian: without holiness, we will be like an astronaut with the best tools but no spacesuit, trying to do the work but lacking the fundamental personal preparation. We can and must pursue the joy of God's salvation; we can and must pursue a consistent life of godliness. Without that, whatever else we might possess, we would simply not have that which is absolutely indispensable to surviving, working, and being fruitful in the role that is committed to us.

Therefore, we need to assess whether the joy of God's salvation and a consistent life of godliness, both in dependence upon the Spirit of God, are our careful, conscious, consistent aim in our praying, studying, and living. Could it be that our relative lack of success as evangelists, individually and as churches, may have at its root the fact that we do not sufficiently manifest the present known and felt realities of divine truth—the joy of God's salvation? Could it be that one reason our witness is not as effective as it ought to be and could be is that the way that we live undoes what we speak with our mouths?

Be Encouraged

Be encouraged by the fact that this is our necessary equipment. We may feel worthless, useless, and terrified; we may be overwhelmed by some of these things. We may stutter, stumble, trip, and shake as we begin to contemplate even the thought of testifying to a sinner, let alone actually going out and confronting one, even if he or she is in our own family—perhaps especially then. We think we have nothing to offer; we would not even begin to open our mouths before the saints of God, let alone others; we think we have nothing to say to anyone. Nevertheless, if you are a sinner saved by the grace of God, knowing and feeling even something of the comfortable realities of true religion, then—even if you think you have nothing to say to the least of the saints and consider yourself to be less than the least of all the saints—you do have something to say to an unconverted man or woman. It may not be much, it may not be what you wish it were, but if you know something of the joy of God's salvation and if you are striving for a consistent life of godliness, however far short you fall of the heights of those realities, you do have something to say.

God says, "Say it, for I am able to give you the soul for which you crave!" You go in dependence upon God. You speak what you can from a flaming heart. Speak with an eloquence born not of the best schools of oratory, not of reading a thousand books, not of long words, but with the true, effectual, genuine eloquence of an enlivened soul, convinced of the truths that it speaks because it knows those realities in itself. That kind of testimony will do more good than the most self-satisfied, self-sufficient performer who ever lived and walked upon the face of the earth. Why? Because it is real. And the earnestness of soul with which we speak bears testimony to the reality with which we deal.

A minister named John Angell James wrote a book called *An Earnest Ministry: The Want of the Times*. It is a study of the worth and value of sincere and earnest pleading. That same quality of earnestness is required in all labor for the salvation of souls. We need not a mere glossy and gilded eloquence, but something sincere and heartfelt. We need something in our eyes and on our lips that persuades people that—whatever else may be the case—we are fixed and steadfast upon the truths that we proclaim to them and that our eternal destiny is staked upon those realities. That will shake the false foundations of the fallen heart.

CHAPTER 3

AM I COMMITTED?
Our Appointed Means

David is speaking as one who has repented of his sins, turning from them back to God. He has cried out to God that he might have a clean heart and a steadfast spirit within him. He has called upon God to keep him in close communion with Him, and he has asked that he might have restored to him the joy of God's salvation, which no man or woman can have who lives carelessly and unrepentantly in sin. He has prayed that he might be upheld by God's generous Spirit, in order that he might then go and sin no more.

On the basis of this, David then cries out to God with a pledge of obedient service, a desire that God would be glorified, not just in David's own redemption but in the salvation of many others. So he says in verse 13, "Then I will teach transgressors Your ways, and sinners shall be converted to You."

We have considered the undeniable obligation for every believer in Jesus Christ to be a brokenhearted evangelist after the model of David. We have looked over our necessary equipment, asking what must be the foundation of our labors in order that our evangelism be effective. For that we went back to verse 12: "Restore to me the joy of Your salvation, and uphold me by Your generous Spirit." We need the joy of God's salvation, a comfortable sense of what it means to have our own sins pardoned, and a consistent life of godliness, so that what we speak is borne out and powerfully confirmed by the way in which we live.

If you want to liken this to a machine, those two things are the source of power. This is where the heat is found to drive the steam engine. But it is not just heat that we need, not just motive force and ability and drive, it is also light. It is not just a matter of battering people into submission by the avalanche of our joy in God's salvation and holiness of our lives. Rather, it is on the basis of those things and building upon that foundation that David says, "I will teach transgressors Your ways."

There is the question of undeniable obligation: Are we willing to undertake this work? There is the question of necessary equipment: How can we be effective in this work? But we must also consider the appointed means. What is it that I should do? How can I consecrate and structure my labors in order to win souls for Jesus Christ? How do I actually go about pursuing the salvation of sinners? We will direct our attention first to the people with whom we have to deal; second, to the mode of our dealing; and, third, to the substance of our dealing.

The People with Whom We Deal

David says, "I will teach *transgressors* Your ways." A transgressor is someone who crosses a line—somebody who has sinned against the Lord's holy law by crossing God's righteously established boundaries. It is such people that David undertakes to teach God's ways. We need to take the good news to those who need it. It is very easy, even as Christians, to "talk a good game" or pray a fervent prayer, even to preach a potent sermon or to express a real desire or intention that sinners would be saved. But unless we are actually engaging with ungodly men and women in or after those things, we are not doing the work of an evangelist. It is necessary, in order to see transgressors turning to God, that we actually communicate with those who are transgressing. We need to speak with those going on in grievous sins as well as those glossy hypocrites who may look fine, but are like those whom our Lord described as "whitewashed tombs"—apparently pure and holy on the outside, but inside entirely unclean, full of dead men's bones. It is necessary that we go into both situations, because transgressors come in every spiritual shape and size. They can be very uncomfortable to deal with. They can be morally filthy, physically repugnant, and in every way aggressive, or they can be very pleasant, "nice" people who just keep you at arm's length. You find transgressors of God's law working in the very highest positions in the land, attaining to the highest levels of society, and you find them among the lowest of the low, crawling in the gutter.

In our Lord's day in Jerusalem, there were Pharisees: the top dogs, the religious elite, who were in their own eyes more holy than anybody else. What were they before God? They were transgressors. And then there were the tax collectors, the prostitutes, the thieves and robbers, the scandalously immoral. They also were transgressors. Jesus spent time and spoke with them both. Those who thought themselves to be something were disgusted that Christ should even deign to be with those who were "sinners," actually to associate with them, having fellowship with the transparently godless. And yet whether they are openly or secretly godless, whether it lies evident to the eyes of others or not, transgressors are those with whom we must engage in order to teach them God's ways. That does not necessarily mean that we all need to go into crack houses or brothels, spend all our time in the worst areas of our neighborhoods, knock on the doors of the most violent and cruel of our neighbors, minister outside the straight and gay bars and clubs and strip joints…but someone needs to. Are these lost people not transgressors in need of God's salvation? Can we bear to restrict our labors to those with whom we are more comfortable because they accord more with our ideas of what Christians ought to be, at least potentially? What did Paul say to the church in Corinth concerning their past? "Do you not know that the unrighteous will not inherit the kingdom of God? Do not be deceived. Neither fornicators, nor idolaters, nor adulterers, nor homosexuals, nor sodomites, nor thieves, nor covetous, nor drunkards, nor revilers, nor extortioners will inherit the kingdom of God. And such were some of you. But you were washed, but you were sanctified, but you were justified in the name of the Lord Jesus and by the Spirit of our God" (1 Cor. 6:9–11).

That some of these Corinthian Christians had been such men and women means that before they were saved someone was willing to go and speak to them as such. Paul was there preaching to those who needed to hear the truth as it is in Christ: he stood before kings, emperors, judges, and rulers…but he also stood before the street workers and the gang members of his day. He did not consider it beyond him to go either to the very heights or to the very depths of society as an ambassador of Jesus Christ. Whether or not they are palatable to us, if people are sinners, if they have sinned against God, they need the gospel: "Go into all the world and preach the gospel to *every creature*" (Mark 16:15, emphasis added). It is not for us to draw the lines about who needs the gospel, or even whom we should like to see in the church. Rich and poor, male and female, whatever their background or previous creed, every kingdom, tribe, tongue, and nation—if they are transgressors, then they need the gospel.

It is therefore necessary that at least some of us start with but go beyond our own neat and pleasant zones of ease and comfort. That is going to be hard for us, because most of us are set in our ways, and it is not easy to deal with people of whose lives and ways we feel utterly ignorant or who may be very distasteful to us or who move and work and speak in a sphere very distant from our own. We may be unable to rise to the heights of some, we may be unwilling in ourselves to sink to the depths of others, but if we are to see sinners saved then we must go after transgressors. In Matthew 5, our Lord says,

> You are the salt of the earth; but if the salt loses its flavor, how shall it be seasoned? It is then good for nothing but to be thrown out and trampled underfoot by men. You are the light of the world. A city that is set on a hill cannot be hidden. Nor do they light a lamp and put it under a basket, but on a lampstand, and it gives light to all who are in the house. Let your light so shine before men, that they may see your good works and glorify your Father in heaven (vv. 13–16).

Is your church a light to the world? Are you the salt of the earth? Is your light shining before men—all men—from the top to the bottom of society? This is not a picture of a church divorced from the world, but of a church divorced from worldliness and engaged with a fallen world for the glory of Christ.

It is no good if the light just shines inward. If you put a lamp up with the shutters down, then the light and heat are merely contained. You need to introduce the light to the darkness in order for the light to be effective. That is what we must be as churches and members of them: we need to engage with lawbreakers who have besmirched God's image in themselves and who have sinned in any of a multitude of ways, whether they are despicable even in the eyes of a fallen world, common unconverted folk, or glossy performers of outward righteousness with all the appearance of morality. They are transgressors. We need to go to them and deal with them as transgressors. Our light—the light of the gospel that we have in Christ—needs to shine into the darkness of this world, and we must carry it there.

John the Baptist was a "burning and shining lamp" (John 5:35), and so must we be. The light is relatively unprofitable when unveiled in a bright place, but it shows itself wholly effective when introduced into the darkness. This world is a dark place, and we must bring the light of the gospel to bear upon those in the darkness, from those in the foul murk of socially acceptable godlessness to those in the dark corners of scandalous iniquity.

Where will you begin? Some may need to begin with their own family, with children, siblings, or parents never yet addressed. Perhaps it will begin with a pleasant neighbor. You might be chatting over the fence or bump into each other on the street. You might have some small service to perform or an offer of help, and you try to find an opportunity to speak a few words concerning the Lord Jesus, commending Christ and the hope you have found in Him. Or there may be someone across the road or down the street that you have not spoken to before, despite countless cheerful waves when you are both out at the same time. Someone might need help caring for his property during one or all of the year's seasons, and you might volunteer. Perhaps you could invite neighbors over for a meal, and the atmosphere in which you give thanks for the food and the conversation over the table and perhaps a brief, warm time of family worship all press home the claims of Jesus. Maybe there is some awkward, difficult, grumpy neighbor, the scourge of the street, gossiped about and sneered at by everyone else. Is this an opportunity to show that Christ's people are different and perhaps open a gospel door? There may be a group of kids who play outside. Perhaps some older teenagers are hanging around. Maybe they congregate in a park. Could you go and chat with them publicly rather than crossing the street or taking a detour to avoid them? Maybe there is a nearby school, and some of the students hang out afterwards because they have nowhere else to go. Will you speak with them?

When we begin to think in terms of going and saying rather than waiting and staying, the possibilities become limitless. Remind yourself that Christ has promised to be with you until the end of the age and then go, and, as you go, make disciples. You cannot go outside of Jesus' jurisdiction, and no situation carries you beyond His sphere of operations. He has promised that by His Spirit He will be with you always, even to the end of the age. You need that assurance, because you may be rebuffed, even repeatedly. Nice, moralistic, middle-class neighbors will throw up their smokescreens, evade the issues, or politely divert the conversation on to other topics. Some people may make fun of you. Some may ask questions without caring much for the answers. Others will become angry, and some will boast of their sinfulness. Some will lose interest after a few minutes, others after a few months. But sow the good seed, and pray God to prepare the ground of people's hearts. And then keep sowing. It is so easy to give up. Sometimes we find ourselves put off by what we deem to be a negative reaction, forgetting that when the gospel comes, it often does bite unbelievers' consciences, and they kick—sometimes hard—against the goads before finally they submit to the righteousness of God. That anger, bitterness, aggression, or some other spiritual venom may be an initial response to the truth pressed home by the Spirit of God in someone's heart. Therefore, press on. Remember that hearts composed of the rubber of self-righteousness often see the gospel hammer simply bounce off, but those hearts of brittle sin and surface antagonism may be the ones that will shatter when that hammer falls. Indeed, this is the best way to breed brokenhearted evangelists!

To be an unforgiven transgressor is to be a most fearful thing. Such men and women have sinned against the holy God. If they have not turned to Jesus Christ, then they need the good news that Christ died for lawbreakers. Our purpose as Christians is to make the light of Christ shine before the world, to speak of the Christ who has saved our souls from our sins, who has redeemed us from sin and death and hell:

we proclaim the praises of the gracious God who called us out of darkness into His marvelous light, as those who once had no relationship with God but are now His people, who had lacked mercy but have now obtained it in Christ (1 Peter 2:9). We do not call men and women lawbreakers so we will be able to look down on them and say, "Ha! We are so much better than you are!" Remember how David approaches them; remember how we are to deal with one another. We come as those who are ourselves sinners. We cannot put ourselves on a pedestal and say, "If only you were like me, you would not need Jesus Christ." Rather, we say, "Because you are like me and I am like you, you also need Jesus Christ." We plead with the unsaved to hear what we say concerning Jesus Christ, that they would take heed and pay attention, that they would consider what we say concerning the One who has ransomed us. This is why we are here as Christians. This is the thing we pursue night and day: the glory of Christ through the salvation of those otherwise on their way to hell. It is our passionate desire.

We want to be better equipped to go into all the world and preach the gospel to every creature, pleading with and exhorting and teaching sinners that Christ is able to save them in order that they might no longer be subject to the wrath and condemnation of a holy God, but might be washed through the blood of the Lamb, Jesus Christ, and so brought into the kingdom of the Son of God's love and made heirs of all the glories of heaven. It is with these men, these women, these boys and girls, that we must deal—transgressors! We must not allow ourselves to be blinded to the reality of lawbreaking either by how pleasant or acceptable they appear or allow ourselves to be scared off by how filthy and depraved they might become.

The Mode of Our Dealing

How do we address those whom we long to see saved? David says, "I will *teach* transgressors *Your ways.*" We are to teach them, and we are to teach them God's ways. Our normal problems in the face of this exemplary declaration are either that we cannot or will not. What is it to teach transgressors God's ways? It is to communicate truth concerning God; it is at the very least to impart information. Teaching concerns the giving of instruction. This is preeminently true of the preaching of God's Word. That is why the preaching of God's Word must be the central element of the witness of any local church, because our Bibles say that it is through preaching that men and women are saved.

Think again of just a few texts from the New Testament that speak of how important it is that people hear the Word of God and are taught what it means to follow after Christ. At the end of Matthew's gospel, our Lord gives the commission to His disciples, and through them to the church:

> "All authority has been given to Me in heaven and on earth. Go therefore and make disciples of all the nations, baptizing them in the name of the Father and of the Son and of the Holy Spirit, teaching them to observe all things that I have commanded you; and lo, I am with you always, even to the end of the age" (Matt. 28:18–20).

In the letter to the Romans, Paul asks, "How then shall they call on Him in whom they have not believed? And how shall they believe in Him of whom they have not heard? And how shall they hear without a preacher? And how shall they preach unless they are sent?" (Rom. 10:14–15). In 1 Corinthians 2, the apostle declared that when he came among them, he had "determined not to know anything among you except Jesus Christ and Him crucified" (v. 2). He was there to teach them about the Savior of sinners. In Galatians 3:2, he talks of the Galatians, who have been bewitched away, as it were, from obeying the truth, people before whose eyes Jesus Christ was clearly portrayed as crucified. "This only I want to learn from you," asks Paul. "Did you receive the Spirit by the works of the law, or by the hearing of faith?" Finally, in 2 Timothy 2:2, Paul further instructs Timothy that the things the young pastor has heard from Paul among many witnesses should be committed "to faithful men who will be able to teach others also."

What is the appointed means of taking the gospel to unconverted men and women? It is teaching. This is true preeminently of preaching, but it must also be true in all our witness to Christ. We are to be teachers of transgressors, not setting ourselves up as if we know it all, but

teaching as humble, personal evangelists. The mode of action to which
we must cling is teaching the truth as it is in Jesus.

You notice that David is very plain: "I will teach transgressors Your
ways." I hope that we are ready to applaud such a declaration, especially if we account ourselves Christians who hold fast to the Word of
God. David does not say, "Perform to transgressors; put on a drama
for them." He does not say, "Water down or dumb down the truth," or
"Whip up a storm of excitement and emotionalism, as if to drive people
into the kingdom of God on a wave of passion without engaging their
minds." When such obvious shortcomings are identified, we can easily
pat ourselves on the back. Perhaps we do not employ gimmicks, nor do
we try to do things that are not ordained by the Word of God. A gospel
choir visiting the UK won the following plaudit from the press: "You
don't have to be a believer to be inspired." What is the problem? You
might be lifted up, your heart might swell within you, you hear those
thumping and insistent rhythms, those soaring voices, and it is all so
beautiful. But what is actually being carried along inside that? Is there
any truth being clearly conveyed? If this was real gospel communication, then unbelievers may well not be "inspired." When Peter preached
on the day of Pentecost, men were cut to the heart (Acts 2:37). When
Stephen preached before the Sanhedrin in Acts 7, the Word of God
came in convicting power to the point at which sinners gnashed their
teeth and stoned him to death, but some of those fiery words perhaps
stuck in the heart of Saul of Tarsus and might have been among the
goads against which he was kicking when he was finally brought to bow
before the enthroned Jesus. When Paul himself preached in Athens,
some showed utter contempt, some showed insipid curiosity, and some
were truly converted (Acts 17:32–34).

So much of what passes for evangelism in our day is simply froth,
aimed not through the mind to the heart and will, but simply at whip-
ping up or playing on carnal emotions. But when we discuss teaching
transgressors God's ways, we are not talking about outward displays
designed to sweep people without any thought into what some imagine
to be the kingdom of God. We are not talking about trying to stir up
mere human passions.

And perhaps so far many of us are in agreement, perhaps ready to pat ourselves on the back and say, "Yes, we are good Christians, we believe all those things, and over my dead body would such crass manipulations come into the church to which I belong." But there is a problem, because David says, positively and definitely, "I will teach transgressors Your ways." And for some of us, our problems perhaps do not lie so much in the things that we would do but in the things that we are *not* doing as individuals and churches. Accepting that we are not "arguing for unreflecting activism, for carelessness and superficiality," Ted Donnelly asks, "Are we in a position to criticize those who are doing imperfectly what we may not be doing at all?"[1] Jim Savastio puts it like this:

> So the other day there was this kid drowning at the local pool. While several could have responded to the flailing, the only one to dive in was this fat, balding man in ill-fitting trunks. The man did a pitiful belly flop into the pool and then dog paddled over [to] the child and somehow managed to pull him to safety. The fat, balding, winded man was nothing in comparison to the many that *could* have saved the child. There was a handsome guard with his nose buried in a book entitled, "Great Rescues through the Ages—the proper manner and techniques to prevent drowning." There were two men on the side arguing about how to best adapt to the water and especially on whether or not to become more like the drowning child in order to reach him. I could go on, but you get the point. When I transitioned from being in the broadly evangelical camp into the solidly reformed camp, I heard and I repeated many criticisms about all the things that are wrong with evangelism today. Many, if not all, those criticisms are valid. There are often things that are lacking in presentation (but even in these cases, God is using these efforts to genuinely save people). Nevertheless, just as the fat man in our parable, there are those who are getting the job done, who are out and about with a zeal for souls, while too many others stand on the sidelines. The

---

1. Edward Donnelly, *Heaven and Hell* (Edinburgh: Banner of Truth, 2001), 58.

question of Jesus that ought to ring in our hearts when we level our scoffing at the "belly flopping" and the "dog paddling" is this, *What do you do more than others?*[2]

This is neither the time for smugness and criticism from the lean lifeguards as they stand on the side sneering at the dog-paddling—the awkward but effective splashing—of those who do not know how to swim like us, nor the moment to complain about the state of the pool, still less to criticize harshly those who are drowning for getting themselves into trouble in the first place. Now is the time to jump into the filthy water and do all in our power to bring drowning people to safety.

When David says, "I will teach transgressors Your ways," he is not saying, "I will debate with sinners and simply give them my opinion—and take theirs—until at the end we agree to disagree." He is not saying, "Just be around sinners, simply hang around as if they will absorb the gospel without our saying a single word." David does not say, "Be nice to transgressors—they'll figure out that you're a Christian and what it means to be saved." David does not say, "Give your side of the story and allow them to give theirs," or "Undertake some kind of 'hit-and-run gospeling.'" We probably all know some curious and distressing examples of this. I recall a situation in which a deeply distressed man visited the church I serve. He had recently lost his wife to death through a terrible illness and had come to church to see if there were answers to his questions and comforts for his soul. One man took a copy of a well-known evangelistic booklet and simply thrust it with little comment into his hand. With barely a further word, the Christian walked away. I am not saying that God could not have used the truth of that booklet to do the soul of that man some good, but he was wrestling with certain issues about his wife's condition before God, and he knew that she was a sinner, and that tract was not given with Christian affection or supported with Christian explanation when an opportunity was given for

---

2. James Savastio, "A Parable in a Pool," *Reformed Baptist Fellowship* (blog), October 24, 2008, http://reformedbaptistfellowship.wordpress.com/2008/10/24/a-parable-in-a-pool.

both. The cold presentation of those truths, it seemed, drove the visitor away. Too often we hope that some tract will do all our talking for us.

More strangely, we hear of visitors to someone's home leaving a tract in the family bathroom in the hope that when members of the family went in they would be obliged to read something, and they might take up the tract. Others leave a tract in someone's refrigerator in the hope that it would be visited soon. We cannot say that it is guaranteed to be a worthless gesture, but it is not properly evangelism. It may be well-meaning, earnest, and sincere, but it is not really teaching transgressors God's ways. We must seek to engage with others person to person. This seems to be where so many of us are falling short as Christians. Too often either we cannot or will not engage with transgressors so as to teach them God's ways. No one becomes a Christian by osmosis, by silent and unwitting absorption of the truth. No one sucks up Christianity just from being around us and suddenly becomes a Christian without being informed of the truth as it is in Jesus. Carrying around a Bible to show yourself a Christian might eventually spark an interest in someone. However, opening it, speaking it, and living it is evangelism, whereas simply having a Bible—however prominently displayed—cannot (in most instances) be more than a preliminary maneuver intended to open the door to closer dealing with a needy sinner.

The mode of our dealing is teaching: we are to be giving instruction. We must therefore engage in clear, reasoned, earnest, persuasive declaration of God's truth to those yet dead in trespasses and sins, and we must do so both by *pattern* and by *precept*.

A Pattern That Teaches Transgressors God's Ways
Everything we do must manifest and bear out the truth we speak. There simply is no room in this world for a gospel of "Do as I say, not as I do." Our sinful lives, our angry words, our aggressive behavior, our rudeness, our insensitivity, our pride—those things can undo or overwhelm our message of peace with God through the death of Jesus Christ. How do you think people feel when they look at you if you have said to them, "Believe in Christ and be saved; when you trust in Jesus you become a new man or woman, you have new motives and new desires,

your behavior changes"? Will they look at you or me and say, "In what way? What's changed?" They will be quick to pick up on our flaws. We might say, "That's not fair, because there are good bits too!" But it is the flaws they will look at, and our reactions to them. And so, in our lives, we must both pursue a consistent pattern of godliness and manifest a genuine gospel response to our own sins. If we profess the truth without practicing the truth, we rob ourselves of all power in teaching transgressors God's ways:

> Christian love is by no means so plentiful as it might be, nor holy living, either. Is not this the thing that weakens the preaching of the gospel—the want of living the gospel? If all the professed Christians who live in London really walked as Christ walked, would not the salt have more effect upon the corrupt mass than the stuff which is now called salt seems to have? We preach here in the pulpit; but what can we do, unless you preach yonder at home? It is you preaching in your shops, in your kitchens, in your nurseries, in your parlours, in the streets, which will tell on the masses. This is the preaching—the best preaching in the world, for it is seen as well as heard. I heard one say he liked to see men preach with their feet; and this is it, "they ought also so to walk even as Christ walked." No testimony excels that which is borne in ordinary life. Christ ought to be glorified by us, and therefore we ought to be like him, for if we are not, we cannot glorify him, but must dishonor him.[3]

The Precepts That Teach Transgressors God's Ways

Upon the foundation of a holy life we are to declare the truth as it is in Jesus. We must be careful in our worship, which is not first for the sake of men. Our worship is for God. It is Him we come to worship; it is Him to whom we give praise and honor and glory. He is the focus, and we come before Him to have dealings with Him, to hear Him, and to respond to Him in praise and prayer, with repentance and faith. To accomplish that we need Him to speak to us, and this He does through the reading

---

3. C. H. Spurgeon, "In Him: Like Him," in *The Metropolitan Tabernacle Pulpit* (Edinburgh: Banner of Truth, 1971), 29:413–14.

and preaching of His Word. So as we engage in the worship of God, all that we do — by the way we do it, by what we say and sing, by how we pray, by what we read, by the manner and substance of our preaching, by our conversations before and after the service — these things must be teaching transgressors God's ways. If there are sinners in our midst who have not yet been saved by the grace of God in Jesus Christ, those people should not be able to deny that they are learning something about God by being among us (compare 1 Cor. 14:25). They are learning something by what we say and the way in which we say it, by the manner in which we worship God. All of our dealings with God ought to be instructive to one another and to others coming in about who God is, what He is, and the way He is. To be among the people of God as they engage in true worship can and should be a converting experience.

But, primarily, this relates to the clear verbal communication of vital truth. We come to know God by hearing about Him: "So then faith comes by hearing, and hearing by the word of God" (Rom. 10:17). Such communication should be as direct, thoughtful, careful, and balanced as possible. When we speak to someone who has been utterly ignorant of who God is and the way God deals with sinful men, he should no longer be able to say, "I am still clueless." The truth may not yet have penetrated to the soul, and in that sense he may be still in darkness, but he has heard the truth. Such a person should be to some degree instructed in God's ways. As humble disciples of the Lord Jesus, who are ourselves scholars in Christ's school, we need to teach transgressors God's ways.

There are multitudes of ways in which we can legitimately do this, many spheres in which we can teach God's truth. We do not need a classroom with a pliant group of unconverted people. The obvious way, already mentioned, is preaching, where men gifted and appointed by Christ and recognized by His church as gospel preachers declare the truth to all who come within reach of their voice and go out to ensure that as many come to hear the truth as possible. We can do it indirectly by inviting friends and neighbors to come and hear the preaching. But it does not need to come from the pulpit alone. We do it when we teach in Sunday school. We do it in our family worship as we open our Bibles to tell our families about the great things that God has done. We do it as we explain the world and its ways to our children or kneel by their bedside to pray at night. We do it in Bible studies or perhaps prayer meetings. We do it over the water cooler or the photocopier, not stealing hours of our employers' time and making them *de facto* supporters of a vocational evangelist, but by natural, easy, occasional testimonies to the fact that Christ is our all in all. We do it in our everyday conversation, over a coffee, at the checkout, spending time with friends. We can do it even in some of the words, phrases, and patterns of speech that we have, as we indicate that certain things are true about God and His ways of dealing with us. We can do it by commenting on what is taking place in the world or musing over a book we have read or a film that we have seen or heard about. We do it over lunch and dinner. We go out with a group of friends and we are not ashamed to speak a word for Jesus while there. If there is some great disaster or great deliverance, we can bring the Word of God to bear upon that situation, so that in the course of that comment or conversation, God's ways are revealed and instruction is given. We write letters or e-mails, cards, and notes to send our thanks or wish good health. We can give gifts of books, we can hand out tracts, we can send CDs to friends, post notes on social media, or mail MP3s or videos or sermon recommendations. You can probably think of a hundred other legitimate means by which gospel truth can be communicated, but—whatever means we find available and appropriate—what we must pack into those things must be the conscious, deliberate desire to instruct sinners in the ways of God. That should not require some great, formal change of gear in our attitudes and actions, as if we mentally put on our Sunday best in order to make some portentous declamation of truth from on high. We are Christians who know the joy of God's salvation, and to speak of Jesus ought to be the spontaneous overflow of a heart full of love for God and for people.

The Substance of Our Dealing

The substance of all our teaching is to be God's ways. To this end we must devote and consecrate all of our God-given powers and abilities of communication.

What does it mean to teach men and women God's ways? It means to declare to them the God that we have come to know as sovereign and holy, merciful and gracious, longsuffering and abounding in goodness and truth, forgiving iniquity and transgression—a God who is good and does good.

We must speak to them of God's justice regarding sin and His mercy for sinners. We must talk of the righteousness, holiness, and might of God. We must speak of the anger of God against sin, and the grace of God with sinners. We must talk of how God has made peace for men with Himself by means of a sacrifice. We must talk of God's electing love and His sovereign power. We should speak of His mercies, talk of His lovingkindness, and profess all His glorious character. We must reveal to people, and press home upon their consciences, the power and wisdom of God displayed in the death of Jesus Christ. We must show them from our Bibles how Christ is the highest and purest revelation of God, how in Him we see all the fullness of the Godhead bodily. We must show them how forgiveness of sins is obtained through repentance from those sins and faith in Jesus Christ. We must show them Christ's sacrifice in the place of His people. We must teach them of a Christ who rose again from the dead on the third day, a Christ who ascended to God's right hand in heaven, a Christ who intercedes for His church, obtaining a blessing from God for His people in accordance with His mercy, a Christ who is still at work saving sinners from sin, death, and hell. We must tell of a Christ who has sent His Spirit into the church to enliven and enlighten, the Spirit who regenerates, opens blind eyes, and indwells the believer so that these things of the joy of God's salvation and a consistent life are made true of those who trust in Jesus Christ. We must speak to them of life from death, heaven and hell, God's grace and glory, and the life of righteousness, peace, love, and obedience for those who put their trust in Christ. We must show them what it means to be translated from the kingdom of darkness into the kingdom of the Son of God's love.

In short, we must speak all that God has spoken to us in all the fullness of its gospel glory, and we must speak it with clarity, biblical balance, integrity, earnestness, and humility, carried along with fervent desire and ardent prayer for the salvation of those to whom we are speaking. We must become teachers of God's ways.

If all that seems overwhelming, then note that David makes a start in only nineteen verses. Is that not what he is doing here in Psalm 51? Granted, David's words here do not cover every detail of the gospel. Nevertheless, it is a comprehensive, though not exhaustive, record of what it looks like for a man to turn from his sins and find forgiveness with God. Spurgeon put the matter simply: "The more of God we proclaim, the more likely is it that sinners will be converted unto God."[4] The more we speak of God—in all the fullness of the revelation that He has given—the more likely it is that we shall see sinners saved. Candlish drives it home:

> It is not your own righteousness that you have to commend to transgressors, but the righteousness of God. It is that very righteousness of God through faith in which you yourself are delivered from blood-guiltiness, and God becomes to you the God of your salvation. Your complete justification in the sight of God,—the perfect righteousness in virtue of which you are justified,—with no concession of his supreme authority, his sovereignty and law, but, on the contrary, with the fullest vindication of all his just and holy claims,—places you on a high ground of advantage.... But plant your foot on the righteousness of God, the God of your salvation; the saving righteousness which he himself has provided, in the person and work of his own beloved Son. Take your firm ground as being righteously accepted in the beloved. Then lay all hesitancy and false shame aside.... Through grace you are emboldened to appear erect and fearless before God. The same grace will make you bold in the presence of men. Then fear not. Shun not to declare to all men the whole counsel of God.[5]

It is God in all His ways, God revealed purely and preeminently in Christ for the exaltation and vindication of His glory in the salvation of sinners, that is our great and glorious theme. While we could turn all this a thousand ways, let us take to heart just three simple things.

---

4. Spurgeon, "Christian's Great Business," 498.
5. Candlish, *Prayer of a Broken Heart*, 76–77.

Engagement with Those around Us

Are you engaging with the men and women and boys and girls around you who need the gospel of God? Are you and I getting to grips with the lawbreakers around us who, without gospel light, will be condemned for all eternity? Are we speaking with our friends and families—parents, siblings, husbands and wives, sons and daughters? Are we speaking the truth in love to our colleagues and neighbors, even strangers with whom we might have occasional contact? Are we developing the relationships that will enable us to communicate God's ways to needy sinners? We are not motivated by an underhand desire whereby we lose sight of a real person with whom we are dealing, ready to cut another notch in our soul-winners' belts as another dehumanized target falls before the force of our holy logic. Rather, when we are engaging with other men and women, whatever our present relationship with them, one of the things we desire and at which we aim is that we might be the means of their learning by instruction and experience God's ways and thereby being converted from their sins.

Commitment to Teaching the Truth

Are you committed, in principle and practice, to teaching the good news as God's primary appointed means for effective evangelism? Are you learning by experience, developing your abilities and honing your skills, taking whatever opportunities come your way to become more proficient in the life business of the Christian? Are you actually *doing* it? Are you speaking with transgressors, step by painful step, over the long haul? We cannot do it all at once. Sinners can be converted in an instant through teaching or after five minutes of gospel instruction. Such is the almighty power of God working by His truth. But it is also by long-term, repeated instruction, so that the weight of truth is built up until the Spirit of God makes it evident that Christ alone can save. Are we engaging, not just in the short term but in the long term and for the long haul, with all our faculties and capabilities, to bring the light of the gospel to those who are in darkness? Is this work borne along by prayers that the Spirit of God would so illuminate the minds and soften the hearts of those to whom we speak that they might receive the truth and be saved?

It must be the truth that we teach. It must be the gospel that we communicate. We must seek to be skillful in the word of righteousness, that we may not pour out poison while imagining that we are administering soul medicine. Again, this is not a matter of extraordinary gift or talent, but a true and simple grasp on gospel truth. We cannot point to false refuges, waste time on empty explorations, or offer false consolations. We cannot preach man's experience or obedience, but rather God's grace in Christ. It is not the things that we should like to be true or hope may be true or wish were true, but the things that *are* true. The great thing is to point sinners to the Savior. When William Carey, Joshua Marshman, and William Ward, the three missionaries at Serampore, drew up a binding agreement with each other in 1805, this was one of their primary concerns:

> In preaching to the heathen, we must keep to the example of St. Paul, and make the greatest subject of our preaching, Christ Crucified. It would be very easy for a missionary to preach nothing but truths, and that for many years together, without any well-grounded hope of becoming useful to one soul. The doctrine of Christ's expiatory death and all-sufficient merits had been, and must ever remain, the great means of conversion. This doctrine, and others immediately connected with it, have constantly nourished and sanctified the church. Oh, that these glorious truths ever be the joy and strength of our own souls, and then they will not fail to become the matter of our conversation to others. It was the proclaiming of these doctrines that made the Reformation from Popery in the time of Luther spread with such rapidity. It was these truths that filled the sermons of the modern Apostles, Whitefield, Wesley, etc., when the Light of the Gospel which has been held up with such glorious effects by the Puritans was almost extinguished in England. It is a well-known fact that the most successful missionaries in the world at the present day make the atonement of Christ their continued theme. We mean the Moravians. They attribute all their success to the preaching of the death of our Saviour. So far as our experience goes in this work,

we must freely acknowledge, that every Hindoo among us who has been gained to Christ, has been won by the astonishing and all-constraining love exhibited in our Redeemer's propitiatory death. O then may we resolve to know nothing among Hindoos and Mussulmans but Christ and Him crucified.[6]

Personal Knowledge of God's Ways

Are you personally proficient in God's ways? Have you yourself truly known what it is to be saved from your sins by such a gracious Redeemer? If you do not, then you really have nothing to say. Here is the root of all: I, as a sinner, have been saved by Jesus Christ. Although I may know little else of God's ways, I know what it is to be a sinner saved by grace. If I can do no more than list the realities of my experience, then I will list them and drop them into every ear in order to make people hear. And—if the root of the matter is in you and you are rejoicing in the joy of it and are advancing in the righteousness of God, developing in consistent holiness—are you possessed, presently and increasingly, of a warm, insightful, careful, balanced, growing knowledge of God in Christ? Are you increasingly in a position to teach transgressors the ways of the Lord God? Do you have a practical knowledge—not a mere head knowledge or just a memory for reciting, but a knowledge in your heart, soul, bones, and life—of what it is to trust in Christ and walk with God and to discern more and more of His glorious ways and works?

Writing to his brothers, Peter said, "Grow in the grace and knowledge of our Lord and Savior Jesus Christ. To Him be the glory both now and forever. Amen" (2 Peter 3:18). Is it true of you that you are growing in the grace and knowledge of Christ? May it prove true, to His eternal glory.

---

6. As cited in *William Carey: Especially His Missionary Principles*, by A. H. Oussoren (Leiden: A. W. Sijthoff, 1945), 276–77.

CHAPTER 4

AM I FOCUSED?
Our Declared Aim

We turn now to our declared aim. What is our goal, our great desire, as we seek to bring God's truth to needy men and women? How we should be focused in order to accomplish our ends? To help answer this question, we can liken the discipline of evangelism to archery. In sixteenth-century England (and for some centuries afterward, though increasingly unobserved) it was a legal requirement that every English-man keep a longbow and practice archery. We are all, to some extent, bowmen in Christ's army, and under the reign of King Jesus, we would do well to keep up our skill in this discipline in which every saint must be engaged. Each of us has a responsibility to learn how to shoot. Our primary tool is our bow of Spirit-worked, Spirit-dependent holiness. That bow of holiness is strung with the bowstring of Christian joy. We have heard a little of what a potent weapon it can be, but also of the necessity that we keep it in good condition. When those two things are brought together in the right strength and tension, we have an effective weapon. With it, we are to loose the arrows of God's gospel truth with which our quivers ought to be filled.

The next question must be this: What is our target? What are we actually aiming at? What are we setting out to accomplish? What is the bull's-eye on the target?

At Whom Do We Aim?

We must remind ourselves of what we have considered before and also go a little beyond it in our understanding. However, before doing so, let us begin with a truism: arrows are there to be *shot*. They are not to be kept in our quivers. The Bible is not given to rest dusty on anyone's shelf, neither is the truth to be left resting upon the page. It is the living Word of the living God. It is active, and we are to be active in taking it forth.

We must realize that our arrows are not merely for display, to be shown off among our peers. It is a delightful thing to hold up an arrow of truth and admire its beauty. For the redeemed of Jesus Christ to see the truth displayed and to feel its point is a glorious, encouraging, humbling and uplifting thing. In what follows, I am not suggesting for one moment that we never need to speak the gospel, in its narrowest sense, to believers. On the contrary, the central truths of our salvation should be regularly and clearly presented in the plainest and most potent form to all men, including believers. By such means our faith is built up, our love increased, and our understanding enhanced. It enables us to strip away all the false foundations of hope and brings us back to the realities of Christ's atoning blood and justification through faith in our Lord Jesus.

Further, with professing Christians, we are under obligation to encourage, rebuke, and exhort, building one another up by means of the truth, with the aim of progress in holiness. The foundation of the house has been laid, and we are now to build one another up in our most holy faith (Acts 20:32; Jude 20). Remedial work is often necessary, some reminders of the things in which we are established (2 Peter 1:12–15). At times a little tearing down is necessary in order that the building up might be sure and true, but we are essentially promoting the onward development of something already and solidly begun. This, of course, makes a difference to the way in which we go about the task.

However, gospel truth is not there simply to be exhibited among the people of God. We are to employ our gospel arrows in witnessing for Christ. The arrows are not merely to be shaken at the enemy, as if to declare, "We have some pretty impressive arrows here—if one of these hit you it would do some damage!" without ever actually shooting any of them. Arrows are there to be loosed. They are to be drawn into the bows, nocked to the strings, and let fly.

Consider a different illustration to demonstrate our particular emphasis in the work of evangelism. When we deal with unbelievers, we are not trying to cultivate cleared ground; we are trying to restore a wasteland to a state fit for cultivation. In cultivating an existing garden, we are working to some extent with nature. You might train up plants, mow the lawn, and develop what is already established. However, we are here confronting a wilderness: we are not working with the new nature, but against the old, sinful nature in fallen people who are at enmity with God. We are not dealing first and foremost with renewed people —even confused and untaught Christians, having nonetheless the root of the matter in them—but with people dead in their trespasses and sins, with what Psalm 51:13 calls "transgressors" and "sinners."

We Must Go to Those in Need

We need to go to these unconverted transgressors and sinners with the gospel. This has already been discussed, but it must be repeated. We need to do far more than merely discuss evangelism or even agree on its importance. Paul was determined and restless to be breaking new ground, advancing into new territory where the gospel had not been preached before (Rom. 15:20). Paul was by no means averse to building up the saints. He maintained contact with the churches he had planted to make sure that they were well instructed and grounded in the truth. He spent two years in Ephesus explaining the whole counsel of God, teaching daily in the school of Tyrannus (Acts 19:9–10). But his desire as an apostle and evangelist was also to conquer fresh territory for King Jesus. He wanted those to whom he preached to receive the truth and to be saved from their sins. His desire was not only and always to be working on building up what was already in place, but often to be going on and laboring in new regions, preaching the gospel where it had not yet been heard. He could write from faraway of his earnest desire to preach the gospel in Rome and of his hopes to use the center of the empire as a springboard for new gospel ventures. In the work of evangelism, we too need to go where the gospel is needed, to places where sinners are comfortable and saints are distinctive. That does not mean a display of thoughtless and unprepared foolishness or an excuse to indulge our own carnality, but rather the carrying of the gospel to those who are in need, so bringing the light into the darkness. It does not necessarily mean each one of us going to the dregs of society, but it does mean going to those who are not Christians. Paul was a pioneer, and so must we be. There are places all around us where the gospel has never been heard. There may be houses only a few doors away from us where the truth of Christ has never come. There may be streets or whole communities that are dwelling in spiritual gloom. There may be families in which no one has ever known the light shining. There may be those who have grown up without ever hearing that there is good news for sinners and that they are sinners for whom there is good news. There are crowds of commuters who are traveling to hell without knowing where they are going or that there is any alternative. There are people on the streets who are walking in darkness. There are neighbors who know you are different, who may even think you are nice, but who do not know of the hope that is within you and may feel it would be wrong to ask. Some doors are hanging open, and some need a good kicking, but many are genuine openings for us to go through.

Sometimes we barely speak about the gospel among ourselves as Christians. How easy it is to go for weeks or even months without stopping to consider afresh those things that bind us together. But if we have no appetite for such truths among those whose palates have been cleansed from the world, if we are so slow to find fresh delight in the realities of the gospel among the redeemed, what likelihood is there of the good news spilling over when we are among the unconverted?

You may know what it is like to summon up all your courage to speak to someone, or you bump into someone and the conversation opens up and you think, "This may be an opportunity!" You start a conversation, perhaps invite him or her to a meeting or offer some literature, and the person to whom you are speaking says, "Oh, that's wonderful—I am a Christian, too!" You might be encouraged to find a brother or sister in Christ, but you might also feel disappointed: "All that effort, and they're already saved!" There is and ought to be a desire to be breaking new ground, reaching new people, men and women who are in need of the gospel. We need to follow hard upon the heels of our prayers in order that we might employ our gospel weapons to win sinners to Jesus Christ.

There can sometimes be a sense of relief in such an encounter with a fellow believer, especially if we are naturally timid and fearful, and it may do both us and the one to whom we speak some good. But we must do more than talk about the gospel among ourselves as believers, and even finding other believers is not the answer, however encouraging. Rather, we must press on to bring the gospel to those who are perishing. It is the sick who need a physician, and it is to them that we must go, taking with us the cure. We cannot teach transgressors God's ways or see sinners converted to Him unless we go to deal with transgressors and sinners, pressing on after our prayers and putting our weapons of spiritual warfare to their intended use, employing the skills and exercising the freedom we learn among our brothers and sisters.

We must remember, though, that these men and women are as much slaves of sin as they are enemies of God. There is a genuine enslavement, a true lostness. They choose darkness rather than light because they are dead in their sins. They are rebels, but that does not mean they are all constantly sinning with a high hand and reveling in their ungodliness. Many are miserable, distressed, lost, or trapped. We are not trying to beat them; we are trying to win them. We are not trying to destroy them, but to save them. How easy it can be to win an argument and lose a soul! Like the Savior Himself, who wept over Jerusalem (Luke 19:41), the brokenhearted evangelist is full of compassion. We have ourselves tasted and seen that the devil is cruel and merciless as well as that the Lord is good. We have known the power of sin and the emptiness of ungodliness. We have eaten of the sand and ashes and dust of this passing world and found that they could not meet our hunger. Broken cisterns could never slake our thirst. But it is only because our eyes have been opened that we can see things as they truly are, and we must remember that awful mastery that sin has over them: "The natural man does not receive the things of the Spirit of God, for they are foolishness to him; nor can he know them, because they are spiritually discerned" (1 Cor. 2:14). Enmity and ignorance, rebellion and darkness mark those without Christ. Those who do not believe have minds blinded by the god of this age, "lest the light of the gospel of the glory of Christ, who is the image of God, should shine on them"

(2 Cor. 4:4). We desire to speak to them in such a way that the light and heat of gospel truth might be brought to bear upon them by the Spirit of God, redeeming them from the power of Satan and bringing them into the kingdom of God's Son.

We Must Understand the Need

In going to such men and women, we need to understand them to be transgressors and sinners. This must be true as we approach them as a group and as individuals. We must remember with whom we are dealing and what they are in their nature. Unconverted men and women are, at root, those who are at enmity with God, however socially acceptably or otherwise that shows itself. There is a fundamental sense in which they are enemies of God, rebels against our great king. Their hearts are against God and His Christ. They want nothing to do with Him. If you peel off all the layers of culture and politeness and get to the root of the matter, you find there a heart that is contrary to God and that wants to go its own way and do its own thing. We acknowledge that there exists what is usually called common grace, that blessing of God whereby people are not as bad as they might be, and many are genuinely kind, friendly, positive, and helpful. However, we must have in mind that at the core, however outwardly and genuinely pleasant they might be and however privileged they are, sinners are rebels against God.

We must remember this in our families, especially as Christian parents in dealing with our children. The privileges of gospel training are incalculable. Our children have been given unusual light; they have been taught and instructed. Children so trained are not "little heathens" in the sense of those who are utterly without any knowledge of God, but mere gospel instruction does not make them half-Christians. While we recognize the blessings of knowing the truth, we must not deceive ourselves or our children. We must still pursue their souls.

While at times Spurgeon's counsel regarding children veers toward the sentimental, in the main thing he is pointed and plain: "So let us constantly pray for our children, that they may know and believe more and more. The Scripture is able to make them 'wise unto salvation' but only 'through faith which is in Christ Jesus.' Faith is the result to aim at:

faith in the appointed, anointed, and exalted Savior. This is the anchorage to which we would bring these little ships, for here they will abide in perfect safety."[1]

How vital it is to grasp this! Too often we fall into the trap of preaching the gospel to adults and the law to children: "God wants you to be good boys and girls." It is not that there is no truth in that statement, but without the right context and qualifications it is a recipe for hopelessness. If you were speaking to an adult, to which of them would you simply say, "This is the gospel: God wants you to be a good person"? That is not good news for anyone! Our children need the pure gospel just as much as any others and are no less capable of receiving and believing it.

Thus our dealings with our children must be with the design of bringing them into God's kingdom as well as equipping them to serve Him in it. Bringing them up "in the training and admonition of the Lord" required in Ephesians 6:4 must have as its first aim their salvation. We cannot afford to turn around Paul's reminders to Timothy: "But you must continue in the things which you have learned and been assured of, knowing from whom you have learned them, and that from childhood you have known the Holy Scriptures, which are able to make you wise for salvation through faith which is in Christ Jesus. All Scripture is given by inspiration of God, and is profitable for doctrine, for reproof, for correction, for instruction in righteousness, that the man of God may be complete, thoroughly equipped for every good work" (2 Tim. 3:14–17). We must grasp that the foundation for teaching, reproving, correcting, and instructing with a view to spiritual maturity is teaching, reproving, correcting, and instructing with a view to spiritual life. Birth precedes growth; faith must necessarily come before life.

So, when we train up our children, nourishing them in every aspect of their humanity, whatever else we try to do in our training (guidance, including physical discipline, toward righteous living) and

---

1. C. H. Spurgeon, *Spiritual Parenting* (New Kensington, Pa.: Whitaker House, 1995), 78.

admonition (implanting the truth into our children's minds, hearts, and consciences), we must seek to bring Christ to bear upon their souls.

Our care of our children must be an expression of the highest love and deepest regard for them. One of the most ardent cries of the book of Proverbs is that of the earnest father: "My son, give me your heart" (Prov. 23:26). All our words and deeds, whether admonition and instruction ("Come, you children, listen to me; I will teach you the fear of the LORD" [Ps. 34:11]) or gracious, loving discipline ("He who spares his rod hates his son, but he who loves him disciplines him promptly" [Prov. 13:24]) ought to be done with the view of delivering our children's souls from death and hell. A man must chasten his son while there is hope, and not set his heart on his son's destruction (Prov. 19:18). In all this we must model God as Father to our children so that they say, "If my father's attitude and actions toward me are a faint reflection of God the Father's toward His adopted children, then I want that God as my Father." Likewise we must, in our marriages, model Christ and His church in our relationships as husband and wife so that our children can say, "If my father's thoughts, words, and deeds reflect what Jesus is toward His church and my mother's thoughts, words, and deeds reflect what the church enjoys from and offers to Jesus, then I want this Jesus as my Savior, and I want to be a part of His church."

When family or friendly relationships are disrupted by sin, we must step in with training and admonition and cultivate and encourage those gospel transactions of forgiveness sought, extended, and received that are the means of reconciliation not only on the horizontal plane (between parents and children, siblings, and others) but also on the vertical plane. The sinner, whatever his or her age, must come to recognize that ultimately sin is sin against God—"Against You, You only, have I sinned, and done this evil in Your sight" (Ps. 51:4)—and that forgiveness must therefore be sought and received from a God who delights to forgive. Everything must be calculated to bring our children to the cross of Jesus, and they must see our own brokenhearted dealings at the cross as a model of the gospel transactions that we desperately desire for them.

This does not imply coaching into formal modes and patterns. Here, John Bunyan is helpful in responding to the qualms of parents who, for example, fear that without putting words and forms into their children's mouths, they will never learn to pray:

> My judgement is, that men go the wrong way to teach their children to pray, in going about so soon to teach them any set company of words, as is the common use of poor creatures to do.
>
> For to me it seems to be a better way for people betimes to tell their children what cursed creatures they are, and how they are under the wrath of God by reason of original and actual sin; also to tell them the nature of God's wrath, and the duration of the misery; which if they conscientiously do, they would sooner teach their children to pray than they do. The way that men learn to pray, it is by conviction for sin; and this is the way to make our sweet babes do so too. But the other way, namely, to be busy in teaching children forms of prayer, before they know any thing else, it is the next way to make them cursed hypocrites, and to puff them up with pride. Teach therefore your children to know their wretched state and condition; tell them of hell-fire and their sins, of damnation, and salvation; the way to escape the one, and to enjoy the other, if you know it yourselves, and this will make tears run down your sweet babes' eyes, and hearty groans flow from their hearts; and then also you may tell them to whom they should pray, and through whom they should pray: you may tell them also of God's promises, and his former grace extended to sinners, according to the Word.
>
> Ah! poor sweet babes, the Lord open their eyes, and make them holy Christians. Says David, "Come, ye children, hearken unto me; I will teach you the fear of the Lord" (Ps. 34:11). He doth not say, I will muzzle you up in a form of prayer; but "I will teach you the fear of the Lord"; which is, to see their sad states by nature, and to be instructed in the truth of the gospel, which doth through the Spirit beget prayer in every one that in truth learns it. And the more you teach them this, the more will their hearts run out to God in prayer. God never did account Paul a praying

was a convinced and converted man; no more will it
...y else (Acts 9:11).[2]

Of course this does not mean that we are not to teach them the truth or have them memorize the Word of God or learn a scriptural catechism. However, we must avoid simply schooling them in a rote rehearsal of things they do not know and feel as if they did know and feel them by personal experience. Rather, we must instruct them with words of truth and the expressions of it that are often God's means of bringing these realities to bear and provide them with patterns for the spontaneous expression of deep-rooted heart experiences and desires when they come.

So we see that, though the sphere (the home) and relationship (parental authority) may differ with regard to our children from those of other gospel work, we bring the same gospel to bear by whatever legitimate means God brings to our hand. In all our efforts to impart the knowledge of God, we must not lose sight of our aim. We are not trying to improve people or merely instruct their minds; we want to see them finally saved. There is no neutral territory in this battle. We are not dealing with people who are halfway to heaven, but men and women, boys and girls, who are hurtling down a dark path to hell. That is why we must go to them. We are not dealing with people who are a little sick and need to be made better. We are dealing with those who are dead and need to be made alive by the power of God in Jesus Christ. When you plead with someone, you are not pleading for mere improvement; rather, you are pleading for the soul, in order that such a one might be kept from damnation and brought to Christ to gain an entrance to heaven.

We need to know and understand this as the nature of our task and the nature of the men and women to whom we go. Otherwise, we risk deluding ourselves, and we will not aim at the right target. No one is rocking easily on a balmy sea, floating between heaven and hell, ready to make a choice when he will. Those who are not Christians, while they

---

2. John Bunyan, "Praying in the Spirit," in *Prayer* (Edinburgh: Banner of Truth, 2005), 45–46.

are almost certainly not as bad as they could be, have a heart that is in darkness, and they desperately need to come to Jesus Christ in order to be washed in the blood of the Lamb so they might be saved. We need to understand the nature of human hearts, the desperate need of the gospel, and of Jesus Himself, in order that people might be saved from their sins.

We Must Identify Specific Needs

However, while we acknowledge this in general, we also need to remember that we are dealing with individual transgressors, and they are not all the same. Looking around, we say that the whole world is fallen into sin: there is none righteous—no, not one. But not everyone is unrighteous in the same way. All may have the disease, but there are a variety of different symptoms, and the cure must be applied accordingly.

We see something of this, for example, within the same family. When parents have several children, they deal with them all as children. They are all in the same fundamental condition of being children, but they have different characters, personalities, strengths, and weaknesses. Therefore no right-thinking parents treat all their children as if they were carbon copies of one another. One child might be very gentle and soft-hearted, easily entreated, to whom obedience seems to come almost naturally; another might be willful, stubborn, and pigheaded. One is easily distracted and given to daydreams, seeming never to hear the simplest instructions; another is focused and listens carefully and follows directions obsessively. One is particularly caught up in the things of this world; another has no concern for the interests of his or her peers. One has a mechanical or practical turn of mind; another is of a more artistic temperament. In the matter of discipline, some children's hearts are so tender that one look or rebuke makes them burst into tears flowing out of a pricked conscience. Others are born, it seems, with hearts (and other parts!) of leather, seemingly incapable of acknowledging guilt. What does the wise parent do? The wise father or mother speaks to a child according to the way he or she is, communicating with the heart according to the particular need, character, and disposition of the child.

So it is when we carry the gospel to individual sinners. All are sinners, but we find them in different states and stages, and we should be discerning in identifying their particular condition and state as unbelievers. Some are stubborn, willful, and aggressive; others show quick and early interest. Some profess themselves to be "spiritual," while others say they have no thought or regard for anything but the stuff of this life. Different fish will bite at different bait, and so we must employ a range of scriptural lures on our gospel hook.

Though all natural men are in need of salvation, that condition manifests itself in different states. Water comes in solid, liquid, and gaseous forms; its environment has an impact upon it. No one would try to catch water, a liquid, in a sieve, but that would work with chunks of ice; in order to fill a glass, you condense vapor, but you melt ice. So it is with sinners in the world: they come from different environments, and those environments have, to some degree, formed them. We need to come to unsaved transgressors and deal with them in the state that we find them, though appreciating the fundamental reality of their transgression.

We must therefore understand men and women to be in need of salvation in general but also discern where they are as individuals, how they think, what they want, what their hearts' desires might be. How do I get in and get the gospel hook caught in their heart? How do I teach them God's ways, using discernment and speaking appropriately? There is a divine rather than worldly wisdom we can and must employ in speaking with people: Paul and Barnabas in Iconium "so spoke that a great multitude both of the Jews and of the Greeks believed" (Acts 14:1). What does that imply? These men, with divinely imparted wisdom, used discernment and intelligence to choose their words in such a way that the gospel had an entrance by the power of the Spirit into the hearts of both Jews and Greeks, to the salvation of a multitude. We need to "so speak" to those with whom we come into contact that they might be saved, if God so wills.

William Taylor used a helpful illustration with regard to preaching. When we bring the gospel to bear, it is not like some great mounted cannon, fixed in position, so that every time a person wanders across the line of fire, we let rip, always in the same direction. If we are gospel witnesses, we have rather a swivel cannon we bring to bear, swinging around, aiming at those with whom we come into contact, directing our fire, bringing the right thing to bear upon the right people. We do not just fire when they come into our field of vision with the same text for every person in every situation, but we bring the gospel to bear upon the individuals with whom we deal:

> The Cross, as [Paul] used it, was an instrument of the widest range and of the greatest power.... I turn [the pulpit] for you into a tower, whereon is mounted a swivel-cannon, which can sweep the whole horizon of human life, and strike down all immorality, and ungodliness, and selfishness, and sin.... You should make application of the great principles that lie beneath the Cross, to the ever-varying circumstances and occurrences of life, and that in such a way as at once to succor the Christian and arrest and convert the sinner.[3]

Do you see Taylor's wisdom? He does not recommend that we simply take up the cross as some indiscriminately blunt instrument with which to bludgeon into submission every sinner who comes within reach. Rather, we must understand "the great principles that lie beneath the Cross" and appreciate how those principles are to be brought to bear upon different men. We are to discern the mercy, justice, wisdom, righteousness, truth, power, and holiness of God that are made manifest at the cross of Jesus, and address those to the particular needs of particular men with that heaven-sent wisdom which speaks in such a way that men might repent and believe.

We Must Teach in accordance with Need

This pursuit of wise and appropriate witness is where knowledge and insight become vital. In John Bunyan's *The Holy War*, when King Shaddai sought to conquer Mansoul, he sent nine captains in total.[4] The

---

3. William M. Taylor, *The Ministry of the Word* (Harrisonburg, Va.: Sprinkle Publications, 2003), 102–3.

4. *The Holy War* is the allegorical story of Mansoul, a beautiful town built

first four sent up were Boanerges, Conviction, Judgment, and Execution. They were men "stout and rough-hewn," says Bunyan, "men that were fit to break the ice, and to make their way by dint of sword,"[5] hard and strong, going with their banners of black and gray and red, and they pounded the walls of the city. Then King Shaddai sent the Prince Emmanuel to the battlefield, accompanied by the captains Credence, Good-Hope, Charity, Innocence, and Patience: "But when they set out for their march, O how the trumpets sounded, their armour glittered, and how the colours waved in the wind! The Prince's armour was all of gold, and it shone like the sun in the firmament. The captains' armour was of proof, and it was in appearance like the glittering stars."[6]

Why did Shaddai and his beloved son do this? This is a picture of God in His divine wisdom, not just battering away with one great weapon, but sending the right men to do the right job. First He sends the shock troops—the sons of thunder. He sends on their heels, in the train of Emmanuel, men of softer countenance. So we too must learn divine wisdom in arraying our gospel weaponry for maximum effect.

We hold back no truth, but we employ all truth plainly, bringing it to bear in a manner calculated to do those to whom we preach eternal good. That will be different for different people. We must hold back none of God's truth but employ it all wisely in dealing with sinners. We must drive at the heart of the gospel and not wander about on the fringes. Abstruse theological topics, matters often beyond the capacity of many of God's people, are rarely the place to begin. For example, what are your thoughts on the relative merits of infralapsarianism and supralapsarianism? We might imagine we understand the debate and even have our own convictions, but if it does not make sense to many Christians, how is it likely to have an impact on someone who has never opened a Bible in her life? Formal disquisitions on fine theological

---

for the glory of its creator and ruler, King Shaddai. The town is deceived by the evil Diabolus and rejects King Shaddai. Mansoul is eventually redeemed by the victory of King Shaddai's son, Prince Emmanuel.

5. John Bunyan, *The Holy War*, in *The Works of John Bunyan*, ed. George Offor (Edinburgh: Banner of Truth, 1991), 3:270.

6. Bunyan, *Holy War*, 285.

distinctions rarely make a quick entrance into people's hearts. Might they? Yes, we gladly acknowledge the Holy Spirit can use any truth of God—even in the matter of infra- and supralapsarianism, though it is not where we might choose to begin—in the salvation of men and women, somehow and somewhere. But these were not the things that Paul dwelt upon when he went to Corinth: "I preach to you Christ and Him crucified." That means much more than is often assumed,[7] but it surely means this if nothing else: we bring to bear appropriate gospel truth in such a way as to win a hearing and a soul, God willing.

Consider, then, your quiver of arrows. Here is a notched shaft that howls as it comes down out of the air: that is the arrow of judgment, which might be used to put the fear of God into someone who has no apparent regard for the prospect of future damnation. There is the silver shaft of mercy to be fired at those who are lost and low and needy. There is the iron-crowned bolt of truth designed to punch through the armor of atheism. There is the barbed arrow of conviction that sticks fast in the hearts and souls of those who say that they have no sin or guilt. There is the piercing, needle-tipped arrow of entreaty, as you plead with men and women, boys and girls to be saved from their sins. There is the blunt arrow of justice, declaring that God will be just either in saving by Christ or in condemnation for those who will not turn to the Savior. There are the golden shots of grace, with which we must constantly pepper our targets. There are the red arrows of Christ's loving sacrifice that must be brought to bear upon hardened hearts.

What does this mean in practice? It means that, with regard both to classes of people and to individuals, we must choose our arrows with care. We have already mentioned how the wise parent gauges the character, constitution, and circumstances of each individual child in bringing the truth to bear. So it is in this wider context. Consider, for example, two very different environments.

Stand with me first in a meeting for senior citizens, in which men and women who belong to a slightly more genteel age gather to hear

---

7. See William M. Taylor's entire lecture, "The Theme and Range of the Pulpit," in *Ministry of the Word*.

the Bible preached and to speak with believers. As you speak to them, you discover that they were well-brought-up, for the most part, often having been sent to Sunday school and even attending church. They are, by contrast with much that they see in the world around them, nice and "good" people, and they know it. Many of them were faithfully married to one man or woman for the great majority of their adult life. They were committed, diligent employees. They have no criminal records and are often considered—with some justification—to be model citizens. They are, perhaps, very religious. Many still go to some kind of church service and would never dream of leaving the building without dropping a few coins at least into the offering. And they think that they are assured of heaven. As you speak with them, you discover this more and more plainly. When you ask them what they are relying on to keep them safe in the Day of Judgment, they assure you of their good record and their good heart. They tell you of all that they have been and done or not been and not done. They point to how much better they are than others.

But there is more even than that. Among these senior citizens, we find one who worked up from the lowest levels of poverty to make a comfortable life for himself and his family. Next to him sits an old lady whose father was a prominent local official when she was a child. One man has been a manual laborer all his life, and his hands still bear the scars and some of the strength of his toil. Another of them went through unspeakable experiences during combat operations. One woman has never traveled more than twenty miles from the place where she was born. Another has been a faithful attendant at religious worship every Sunday since she can remember. She was jilted on the day of her wedding, and never married. Another saw through the hypocrisy of what he thought was all religion when he was young. That gentleman was the local lothario, a smooth ladies' man flitting from flower to flower without ever finding satisfaction. And all of them—with their various backgrounds, experiences, virtues, and vices—are going to hell.

Then, several hours later, come with me to the streets outside the same place where these older men and women meet. There is a gang of teenagers. Most of them come from broken homes, and few of them are interested in being in those homes, at least not until cold and extreme weariness drive them back in the small hours of the morning. They are well-stocked with alcohol purchased from various careless local stores or brought from home. Several of them are smoking heavily, and it is not all tobacco. Their hearts and conversations are full of filth and aggression. They are bursting with vigorous and sometimes violent energy. Some of them are just hanging out. Some of them are looking for trouble. Some are already world-weary, looking for and expecting nothing from life, although some have dreams of winning a television talent show and entering into a life of ease and luxury. Apparently their teachers hate them; they certainly hate their teachers. Several of them are well known to the local police, even if they have avoided a criminal charge so far.

We spend time for a while with that gang of teenagers on the street, and we find that one is a bright boy from a wealthy home whose parents could not care less where he is and who finds his companionship here. Another is the youngest brother in a family of petty criminals following a well-worn path. That girl was abused by her father and by almost every boy and man she has known since. This one has succumbed to peer pressure but is clearly out of her depth, even in this relatively mild environment. That fellow is all bravado, desperate to be the center of attention. This one is all energy, just looking for a buzz wherever it can be found and thriving on the visceral thrill of the latest misdemeanor. And they too are going to the same hell.

We could move on. We could go to the bars and clubs in town to watch older teens and young men and women in their twenties and thirties strutting like the mating animals they are told they are, preening and displaying. And then we can watch as the alcohol-fueled brawls and scuffles break out. Or we can go to the wine bar after work, where the well-paid and well-dressed men and women whose every breath oozes selfishness are congregating to display their well-oiled credentials in a different setting. From there we make our way to a local charity, where tireless volunteers are pouring time and energy and resources into some worthy cause. Or we go into the homes of those worthy causes and find old men and women abandoned by their children, or children neglected, despised, or beaten by their parents. We go into some churches and we find gilded hypocrisy alongside absolute and aimless sincerity. In other religious communities of other faiths we find the same sort of committed and sincere individuals hoping to earn some version of a heaven next to the same charlatans who are seeking to hide their sins beneath a religious veneer. We walk along the road, passing the old lady beloved of her family, the old gentleman abandoned by his, the unmarried couple whose family is and may always be sustained by the state, and the model family who are going up in the world. Further on is the broken home where the mother and son survive quite cheerfully while the father has moved in with the woman across the street. All the variety of sin and common grace and need and greed and vain hope and utter hopelessness, every shade of social and cultural and religious status and standing, and we see so much of it.

We need to bring the cross to bear on every person, to make known the power and wisdom of God in a crucified Christ, who by His death and resurrection has secured pardon for sins and life everlasting for sinners of all kinds. It is the same gospel in every instance, but the brokenhearted evangelist is concerned to discern and then apply that gospel in the most winsome and effective way:

> For though I am free from all men, I have made myself a servant to all, that I might win the more; and to the Jews I became as a Jew, that I might win Jews; to those who are under the law, as under the law, that I might win those who are under the law; to those who are without law, as without law (not being without law toward God, but under law toward Christ), that I might win those who are without law; to the weak I became as weak, that I might win the weak. I have become all things to all men, that I might by all means save some (1 Cor. 9:19–22).

The brokenhearted evangelist does not invariably start from the same point with the self-righteous as with the scandalous, and he adapts to his circumstances. He presents the same truth with a different vocabulary, in a different environment, perhaps wearing different clothes, at a different time of day, in a different place. He is always himself, and his message of salvation through faith in Jesus Christ is fixed, yet he is flexible, ready to adapt in whatever ways are legitimate to bring that gospel to bear, and ready to bring the gospel to bear by all appropriate means and in a variety of legitimate ways.

The woman offended that wicked people get to heaven demands a different approach to the one who wonders how she herself can get to heaven. The young man who is filthy and proud of it might not be addressed in precisely the same way as the old lady who has led a life insulated from sinful excess and indulgence. The sinner reveling in his sin needs the same medicine as the sinner sick of iniquity, but the mode of delivery may differ. You offer food to the hungry friend with whom you are sitting in a different way to the hungry stranger whom you are meeting for the first time. The desperately lonely may be attracted for a different reason to the person with a circle of good friends. The atheist, the Buddhist, and the Muslim must all be addressed with the truth as it is in Jesus from a heart of love, but often from a different angle. The nominal religionist and the sincere but lost each require a different approach. Some need to be encouraged; others might need to be shocked. Some need to be walked toward the kingdom by a friend; others need to be shown the path and left to travel alone to the cross.

From the pulpit there is sometimes necessarily a broader stroke of the gospel brush, trusting that the Spirit of Christ will bring it home to those to whom we speak, perhaps tailoring some part of a sermon, making some particular application designed to press home the truth to those of a certain inclination or conviction. Speaking to a distinctive group, we mold not the essential message but the manner in which we present it, displaying the necessity of salvation to these particular sinners; in person we can do some of the detail work, carefully unpacking the truth, removing the individual defenses and excuses, blowing away the personal smokescreen, and pressing home the truth to the conscience of the person into whose eyes we are looking.

In ancient Israel, when a man was guilty of blood because of negligence, the Lord appointed cities of refuge to which such a sinner could flee in order to escape the punishment that would otherwise be righteously meted out by the avengers of blood. To which sanctuary would the guilty man flee? Why, the nearest one! So it is with Jesus. He is all that a sinner needs, but that awareness of need sends a man flying to the closest true refuge. So the brokenhearted evangelist holds out Christ in all the magnificent richness of His person and work. One flees to avoid impending judgment, finding that Christ delivers from the wrath to come; one because conscience gnaws tirelessly and Jesus grants peace; another because he knows himself dead and finds life in Christ; another because he is friendless and Jesus offers true and saving friendship for time and eternity. The man who has trusted no one since he was betrayed by a friend finds in the Lord one to whom he can entrust his soul; the one who has always sought for purpose in life finds it in loving and serving the Savior of sinners.

If we are to be such witnesses, we must use the weapons God has provided. Our Bibles are our quivers, and we must learn to pull from them the arrows that are needed for the situations in which we find ourselves. We must pursue the souls of men by God's appointed means. It is always the same gospel, but it may find a different entrance. We cannot afford to tickle listeners' ears with irrelevancies; we are not here to speak to them of things they do not need to know. We are not here simply to socialize with them, merely to enjoy our time with them, although that is not wrong in itself. But can you not become a gracious gospel hunter, choosing the weapon for the task, necessary and appropriate truth, in order that by any means you might win some? Like a good hunter we must aim at their hearts with necessary truths: "And I, brethren, when I came to you, did not come with excellence of speech or of wisdom declaring to you the testimony of God. For I determined not to know anything among you except Jesus Christ and Him crucified" (1 Cor. 2:1–2).

This is Paul referring to his first entrance to the Corinthians, now believers but then outright sinners. "What was my determination when I came?" asks Paul. "Not with enticing words of men's wisdom, to tickle your ears, but the gospel according to your true need, being all things to all men, that by all means I might win some." Paul held out Christ in all His multifaceted glory, adapting himself to his audience, and pressing home the one Savior to the hearts of all.

What Must We Aim At?

You probably know what an archery target looks like, with its concentric circles of white, black, blue, red, and bull's-eye of gold. What does an archer aim at? Is he content with merely hitting the target as a whole? Though it all constitutes the target, the archer aims for the bull's-eye. There may be many circles on the target, but there is only one point at which he truly aims. Though he may be relieved at hitting the target, if he misses the bull's-eye, he has missed his mark. When we shoot our gospel arrows, what are we aiming at? As we look at our target of the unconverted person, how might we understand these concentric circles in terms of our particular goal?

The White Ring of Self-Referential Evangelism

Our aim in preaching or speaking the gospel is not to draw attention to ourselves. What would happen if you shot an arrow with a firework attached to the shaft that you lit before loosing it? It might be a screamer, with lots of smoke and sparks. You can be assured that everyone would look to see who had fired; many people might be impressed with your noisy, sparkling arrow, but it would not go anywhere near the bull's-eye. The point of shooting an arrow is not to draw attention to yourself—not even to admire the arrow itself. The point is to hit the target, and we will always miss if we shoot with reference to ourselves and our own esteem, to what others will think of us, even with unconverted people with whom we might like a reputation as good Christian men or women. Perhaps we speak the gospel simply to assuage our own consciences, without any particular desire beyond that. We might hope that other believers will esteem us because of our courage and boldness. We might even get a reputation among unbelievers as someone of integrity and conviction and be pleased by it.

But that is not our aim, not our desire. We aim at the conversion of sinners to the glory of God in Jesus Christ, and unless we hit that target we are disappointed and distressed. We want to see people saved—obtaining life from death, leaving behind their sin and turning to God with a Spirit-fueled, whole-souled embrace of Christ, to the praise of His glory. Nothing else will do. When Paul was before Felix and Herod

Agrippa (Acts 26), Herod was "almost persuaded" to become a Christian (v. 28). Paul said, "I would to God that not only you, but also all who hear me today, might become both almost and altogether such as I am, except for these chains" (v. 29). Paul's desire as a preacher to those men was not that they be almost Christians, waiting on the periphery or dancing on the fringes, but altogether delivered. We want people to be altogether Christians, not dribbling in, but leaping with open arms to embrace Christ. We will take them crawling, but we want to see them come running—men and women wanting to give themselves wholly to the service of God out of love for Him.

In one sense, there is as much value in hitting this ring as there would be in shooting ourselves in the foot. We have far from accomplished our aim if the only ones to benefit from the activity are we ourselves, in our petty pride and cowardice.

The Black Ring of Social Acceptability

To some degree, the gospel does have a civilizing effect, but are we concerned only with the reining in of a person's more public sin and scandalous behavior? Is it sufficient to have sin controlled or restrained to some degree, without any deeper penetration? There are some curious photos of Victorian missionaries in the African bush. They were faithful men and women who sacrificed much, but some of the photos still amuse. Arrayed around them in the bush are the black African tribesmen and women, fully clad from neck to toe in ornate Victorian clothing, with some of the men still holding their spears. The ministry of the missionaries had an evident, outward, civilizing effect. Those people are dressed to enter polite Victorian society, except for their spears.[8] So it is possible to clothe sinners in respectable garb but leave them clasping the weapons of their rebellion. We are not trying to equip people outwardly to look better in society while leaving them holding the spear of enmity against God. Are we out simply to make vile sinners

---

8. This is not a comment on their salvation, merely on their appearance, by means of illustration.

into socially acceptable sinners? No, if that is all we accomplish, we have missed the mark.

The Blue Ring of Good Citizenship

Good citizenship is a little nearer to the mark, perhaps, but is it really enough that men and women be sober, honest, decent, hardworking, faithful to spouses, and loving toward their children? These are not negligible things by any means, but neither are they our goal in and of themselves. We do want to see lives reformed, but however much we desire morality and reformation in people's lives, that in and of itself— without springing from a changed heart—should not be our aim.

We must neither compromise our message to accomplish this end alone nor rest satisfied with this as the acceptable fruit of the gospel itself. It can seem like a great stride forward to see the grosser manifestations of godlessness eroded and a pattern of self-control, good neighborliness, civic responsibility, and social dignity cultivated. But if you unpack the layers, you might find beneath that outward morality an enduring hostility to Christ, especially when you get close to people's particular sins. And so it is not enough to preach good behavior, calling for that which an unregenerate person, by dint of a little effort, can accomplish in his own strength. The flawed assumption of so many people is that true religion is about nothing more than being "nice" and "good," and—while there is nothing inherently wrong with niceness and goodness—our teaching must make plain that conversion penetrates far deeper, accomplishing genuine holiness from the inside out.

It is not enough to make people good citizens. There are instructed people in the world, manifesting a degree of common grace and willing to accept and even to commend some of the outward norms of Christian morality. Many still want to be thought of as upright and moral citizens, with a code of ethical conduct, after a fashion. Some are very proud of this reputation. Others believe that the veneer of cultural religion provides an appropriate gloss to a moral life. They are not openly hostile to the truth until closely pressed, at which point, very often, their animosity toward true, vital religion is revealed. It is when we suggest that the moral or religious are sinners in need of a savior that the hackles rise! Here is the pillar of the community, a businessman of good standing, perhaps an occasional churchgoer. His wife no longer needs to work but is a volunteer at any number of worthy causes. Their garden is neat; their home is clean; their credentials are impeccable; their children are all of the above. And we could mold sinners into this form and leave them lost for all eternity, for such men and women may remain in desperate need of salvation through faith in Jesus.

We must ensure, therefore, that the gospel that we declare does not allow those to whom we preach to rest easy in a culturally conditioned pleasantness of outward demeanor. We must dig beneath the surface, probe the depths of the soul, and make plain that God desires truth in the inward parts (Ps. 51:6), not merely in the outward. We must be clear that our gospel aims require far more than the securing of a greater conformity to "Judaeo-Christian ethical norms," and we cannot allow transgressors to imagine that such outward conformity is sufficient to bring them into the kingdom of God.

The Red Ring of Good Churchmanship

Moving onward and inward, what if we were able even to persuade men and women to be church members, so that they could sit among us without appearing to be anything less? Is it enough to be as Cornelius or Lydia were before they were converted? They are described as devout, God-fearing worshipers and alms-givers. What of the Ethiopian eunuch when he first met Philip? He is there in his chariot, having found a way as his vehicle bumps along the road to be earnestly reading in the prophet Isaiah. Such men and women may keep company with God's people, and they are often exemplary in their behavior. You might rather have an unconverted Cornelius or Lydia in the congregation than some of the Corinthian believers. Cornelius fits the bill, we think, but let's not touch the Corinthians. But is this sufficient? Those who appear to fit into the church may have no true part of Jesus Christ. If all we accomplish is to have men and women fill their places in the pew and the coffers of the church, going through the motions of public worship without their hearts ever being won to Jesus Christ, we have missed the mark. It is not enough to fit seamlessly among the members of Christ's church, melding—being absorbed—into the atmosphere of Christianity without experiencing the reality of it. If we labor only to form those who *fit into* without being *part of* Christ's church, we fall short.

Again, it can be easy, even on account of weariness and disappointment, for the brokenhearted evangelist to stop short of salvation. We may mistake—even sincerely—good churchmanship for true conversion. In each of these rings of social acceptability, good citizenship, and good churchmanship, we must recognize the difference between merely a leashed animal and a genuinely tame one, between a wolf—whether or not in sheep's clothing—and a sheep. Our teaching of God's ways must make plain that the nature, and not just the appearance, of the wolf must be forever carried off. That teaching must also be of a character that sets out to bring about salvation by pressing those distinctions into the conscience. We must therefore go to our Bibles to discern what genuine conversion and true discipleship look like, sound like, and act like. We must recognize that true Christianity consists in *a humble and wholehearted embrace of the divine diagnosis of and remedy for sin, a humble reverence for and joyful devotion to God and His glory,* a principled pursuit of godliness with an increasing attainment in holiness, and an abiding affection for and attachment to God's redeemed people. Then our declaration of God's ways should uncover anything parading as Christianity that is less than and other than this, exposing it for vanity and grasping for the wind, and should aim only at the proper root of heart consecration to God and the genuine fruit of godliness as the outworking of the Holy Spirit's ongoing operations in the life of those redeemed by Christ's blood.

While we recognize that there are degrees of sanctification among the truly saved, there is in one sense an absolute difference between common grace and saving grace, and our labors for God, in their aim, design, and distinctions, should make that clear. It is tragically possible to live and die a model citizen and a condemned sinner. We must not be first concerned with the appearance but with the heart. We must not pursue a mere reformation in behavior, but a genuine renovation of the soul. Some, for reasons of incipient Pharisaism or because of misguided good intentions, become more concerned to bring sinners into conformity with some of the normal cultural effects of Christianity than into conformity with Christ. The danger is that we shall aim at, accomplish, and be satisfied with only the molding of the outer man while neglecting to address the inner man.

So suppose a junkie walks in off the street hoping to turn his life around and appreciates the kindness shown by the people of God. They offer food, water for washing, clothing, and help to get him back on his feet. He kicks his habit quite readily, with few lapses, and gets a good job. Within a few years he is considering marriage, buying his own home, driving a nice car. Every Sunday he takes his seat in the place of worship, having learned to sing in praise and bow his head in prayer. He is polite, friendly, settled, and mature. He tithes to the local church and supports local charities. He may vote for what is considered the right political party. He is a model of outward reformation. But he may still be going to hell. He may fit the bill of civilized Christianity and still be far from heaven. He has never been truly changed. And one day, the faithful preaching under which he has been sitting uncovers a sin that has never been touched before. Perhaps it may even be his satisfaction with the very life that he has created for himself. His unsubdued heart rises up in fury that anyone should call a man like him a sinner, and he vows never to darken the doors of that church building again.

But suppose another junkie walks in off the street and hears the same gospel. His heart is truly pierced. He leaves without speaking a word to anyone but heads back to his sleeping bag under the local railway line and cries out to God for salvation, and God in mercy hears him. He never gets a job that he can hold down. He could never afford to remove his tattoos even if he were to wonder whether it might be a good idea, especially with some of the more vulgar ones. He never takes out any of his multiple piercings. He tries to get off drugs but has frequent relapses. He comes to church quite a lot, and he is given food and clothing and water to wash and shave and often turns up the next week in much the same condition as before. He can barely read, and he loses the Bibles he is regularly given with equal regularity. Life is a constant battle that sometimes goes better but often seems worse. His patterns of speech and behavior cause regular and painful conflicts with others in the church. He is a drain on the resources of the elders, the deacons, and those in the congregation who try to invest in him. He rarely remembers to thank them. Church discipline has been enacted in varying degrees times without number, and on each occasion he has come back, but even the most optimistic wonder when the cycle will begin to repeat. But he is constantly seeking and being granted forgiveness, and under the faithful preaching of the Word of God, and with the loving witness of the saints, inch by painful inch he scrapes forward toward heaven, repenting and believing, though the life of this saved man seems only marginally less messy on the day of his death than it was on the day he was born again.

Now, which is ideal? Clearly neither, but the man in the second illustration will go to heaven while the first, unless he is humbled and submits to the righteousness of God, will end up in hell. If we are honest, until the point of crisis arrives in the experience of the first man, we might very well have assumed—and with good and legitimate grounds—that the person in question was a genuine brother in Christ. We might also have sometimes questioned—again, on good and legitimate grounds—whether or not the second individual was truly saved. The answer in both instances is to go on teaching God's ways in what a former generation of Christians would have called a discriminating fashion. That is, we must not fail to make plain the difference between nominal and damning and real and saving religion, to go on pressing into the hearts of all who hear us the sole sufficiency of Christ, the emptiness of good works as a means of obtaining salvation, and the necessity of good works as a means of demonstrating salvation, challenging and probing graciously but honestly to ensure that the root of the matter is truly in us and in others. We must call constantly, urgently, penetratingly, for "repentance toward God and faith toward our Lord Jesus Christ" (Acts 20:21). We must consider not only what a man has attained to, but from where he began and where he is truly going. To be sure, the above example is a little extreme, but our danger is that we may major on and rest satisfied with mere outward conformity to the norms of a cultural Christianity and neglect in some cases or miss in others the reality (or otherwise) of a saving relationship with the only Redeemer of sinners. The brokenhearted evangelist may be often bewildered by, unsure of, and even disappointed with the results of his work, but he knows that at which he aims, and he is never willing to aim anywhere else.

So there is a further question for every reader. You may be a socially acceptable person. You may be an outstanding citizen. You may be a member in good standing of a gospel church. You may even be prominent in your zeal to see sinners saved. But are you a Christian? Everything else is insufficient, even empty, without this. None of us can afford to rest with mere outward reformation, with being a weeping Ahab or a remorseful Judas or a seemingly generous Ananias or an almost-persuaded Agrippa or an earnest Simon Magus. We must accept that certain norms of acceptability in a particular society or culture, or some part of it, may be lacking where the righteousness of Christ clothes the soul, but, by the same token, we must not neglect either the blessed realities of justification or the necessary consequences of sanctification in seeking the salvation of the lost. There will be those who cry out in the judgment, "Lord, have we not prophesied in Your name, cast out demons in Your name, and done many wonders in Your name?" (Matt. 7:22). And Christ will answer, "I never knew you; depart from Me, you who practice lawlessness!" (v. 23). Let us not confuse civic acceptability with true righteousness, the laws of men with the law of God, social order with spiritual life. And let us ensure that having preached to others, we are not ourselves cast away.

The Bull's-Eye: Conversion to Jesus Christ

"Almost" will not do! We want people to be altogether delivered, saved from their sins by the grace of God. We do not draw our bow at a venture in the hopes of hitting home—we aim at the hearts of unconverted men and women. We do not want them simply to be nicer, better, or even more regular in their attendance, but we wish to see them saved from their sins by Jesus Christ to the glory of God the Father. Nothing else satisfies. All else, however commendable, is still a falling short: we aim at people's hearts with gospel truth. Do you know what you want to see taking place when you bring the gospel to bear upon an unbeliever?

Do you have an intention and an expectant hope in your heart? Do you go after that person graciously but sincerely, in order that she might be saved? Is that what you are driving at, and are you legitimately disappointed if that does not happen? When the preachers of God's Word stand in the pulpit and speak the gospel, are you satisfied when visitors come in unbelievers and walk out unbelievers? Are we simply displaying our oratorical skills—or lack of them? Are we showing how much we know and giving our opinion, or do we want to see salvation—men and women redeemed by the power of God? Evangelism is not merely an exercise in church publicity. We reach out so that people might be saved! That is the great mark at which we aim, and we are dissatisfied unless we strike gold. Here the analogy fails: an archer obtains points for the colored rings, but Christians, in one sense, achieve nothing of real, eternal value unless and until they see a person saved.

This is the object of our labors: we desire God to be glorified in the salvation of sinners, and to that end we speak, preach, write, invite, and pray. We will be grievously disappointed if weeks and months, let alone years, pass without sinners being saved in our midst. Is this not God's gospel that is preached? Is this not the power of God to salvation for everyone who believes? We do not preach it for display or simply to declare our presence. We preach with purpose: the salvation of sinners, from the very beginning of their spiritual lives until they are safely delivered into the eternal presence of Jesus Christ.

As we evangelize, is this our declared aim and constraining desire? Is this what we are aiming at and hoping for in our witness to Jesus Christ? Is this our expectant hope, or has a lack of fruit dented our sense of anticipation? Will we be satisfied with anything less than the supremacy of Christ displayed in the salvation of sinners? This is what we desire: the church of Christ built up, the glory of God revealed, the power of Jesus Christ demonstrated as He plucks sinners from every strand and stratum of society, from top to bottom, from east and west, making them His own to the praise of His grace.

Counsels for Shooting Arrows

To this end let us *labor to keep our bow and bowstring serviceable and in good condition*. Is your bow well cared for, the stave protected from all that would crack, dry, or damage it, making it unsuitable and unserviceable in the cause of Christ? Are you keeping the bowstring safe from the spiritual damps that rob it of tension, so that it is no longer effective for the shooting of gospel arrows? This is a matter of holiness and zeal. Nothing equips us better for this work than walking humbly with God, and nothing more quickly unfits us than casual carnality and carelessness with regard to sin. It is those who know their God who are strong and do exploits (Dan. 11:32), and this is a heart knowledge, a maintained communion with Him. Go back to what we said about the joy of God's salvation. Remember again that counsel from Robert Murray M'Cheyne:

> Do not forget the culture of the inner man,—I mean of the heart. How diligently the cavalry officer keeps his sabre clean and sharp; every stain he rubs off with the greatest care. Remember you are God's sword,—His instrument,—I trust a chosen vessel unto Him to bear His name. In great measure, according to the purity and perfection of the instrument, will be the success. It is not great talents God blesses so much as likeness to Jesus. A holy minister is an awful weapon in the hand of God.[9]

What is true of the gospel minister in his particular duties is true for all saints in theirs. M'Cheyne, and others who have spoken like him, have never suggested that somehow a cultivated holiness is means of twisting God's arm until He blesses us. Nevertheless, there is a definite connection between the holiness of the vessel and the use to which it is put. Again on the words, "If the Lord delights in us, then He will bring us into this land and give it to us" (Num. 14:8), Andrew Fuller said, "The term *delight* does not express that Divine love to our souls which is the source of our salvation, but a complacency in our character and labours.... The amount is, that if we would hope to

9. Andrew Bonar, *Memoir and Remains of Robert Murray M'Cheyne* (1892; repr., London: Banner of Truth, 1966), 282.

succeed in God's work, our character and undertakings must be such as he approves."[10]

To discuss this at great length is outside the scope of this work. Suffice it to say that without careful, cultivated, consistent godliness—living in the fear of the Lord, in dependence upon the Spirit of the risen Christ—we will never be in a fit state for sustained effectiveness in the shooting of gospel arrows. Gospel success is not so tied to personal holiness that God's sovereign purposes to bless whoever He will by whomever He will are somehow bypassed. If God took account of our sinful failings in granting blessing, which of us would ever anticipate the least gospel success? However, that God can and sometimes does overrule in these matters does not allow us to neglect M'Cheyne's general principle that "in great measure, according to the purity and perfection of the instrument, will be the success."

Let us then pursue holiness in the fear of the Lord, employing all the appointed means of grace, investing in and profiting from Christian fellowship, seeking the face of God, delighting in His truth, developing a habit of true communion with Him in meditation and prayer, keeping short accounts with Him, and putting sin to death wherever and whenever it breaks cover in our lives. Ask God to grant that you may keep yourself in a fit condition to bring the gospel to bear, and depend upon Him in pursuing such an end; pray that He might affirm in your own heart the gospel truth concerning Christ to stir your own soul to love and adore Him.

Let us also fill our quiver with serviceable arrows, well chosen from the armory of God's Word and able to be employed. Have you been searching your Bible so you will know how you might deal with sinners of different stripes? Are you ready to use your arrows, so that at a moment's notice you might let them fly? By hiding the Word of God in our hearts, we are not only kept from sinning against Him ourselves (Ps. 119:11), but we are equipped to bring the good news to others: "For the weapons of our warfare are not carnal but mighty in God for pulling

---

10. Andrew Fuller, "God's Approbation of Our Labours Necessary to the Hope of Success" in *Complete Works*, 1:188.

down strongholds, casting down arguments and every high thing that exalts itself against the knowledge of God, bringing every thought into captivity to the obedience of Christ, and being ready to punish all disobedience when your obedience is fulfilled" (2 Cor. 10:4–6).

When Paul speaks elsewhere of the Christian's battle gear, he identifies a primary weapon: "the sword of the Spirit, which is the word of God" (Eph. 6:17). There is nothing that we need more than to have the Scriptures at our fingertips in this battle. Whether we are in the pulpit, alongside someone in the pew, chatting to a friend, speaking to a group, or explaining to a child, we need to have the Word of the living God ready to be employed in an appropriate context and with an accurate sense. We must store our minds with the truth and feel its power in our hearts so that we can bring forth those particular truths in their particular forms that are best suited to the needs of the moment. To return to William Taylor's metaphor, there is little inherent power in mindlessly hammering away with, say, the mantra of John 3:16. Again, that the Lord can take what truth He will and use it how He will we never deny, but we remember once more that Paul and Barnabas "so spoke that a great multitude both of the Jews and of the Greeks believed" (Acts 14:1). Jeremiah was given his marching orders by the Lord:

> Behold, I have put My words in your mouth.
> See, I have this day set you over the nations and over the kingdoms,
> To root out and to pull down,
> To destroy and to throw down,
> To build and to plant (Jer. 1:9–10).

You notice how the Word was given to accomplish the whole range of his prophetic ministry. There is a time for rooting out and pulling down, for destroying and throwing down, to wreck false hopes and uncover cherished sins, to expose foolish notions and to humble proud hearts: "'Is not My word like a fire?' says the LORD, 'And like a hammer that breaks the rock in pieces?'" (Jer. 23:29). There is what older writers called "law-work," as the weight of God's holy law in all its terrible spiritual pressure was felt in a person's heart, as the Ten Commandments were pulled like a harrow across his soul to plough up the too-placid surface of his life. The brokenhearted evangelist knows when to fire arrows for this work. But when the breaking is done, then the balm of Gilead needs to be poured into the wounded soul: "Come," said Hosea, "and let us return to the LORD; for He has torn, but He will heal us; He has stricken, but He will bind us up" (Hos. 6:1). Here the medicine of the gospel is poured into the sin-sick heart. So it is with God's faithful witness: he knows when the time has come to point the way to true comfort, to hold out the saving mercies of God in Christ with tender freeness and loving clarity.

An example of this sensitivity is seen in the ministry of Daniel Rowland, one of God's firebrands in the evangelical awakening in Wales in the eighteenth century. In the first days of his ministry, Rowland—only lately awakened to divine realities himself—is described thus:

> What he preached at first was the law, in its high and minute demands, and in its awful threatening. He stood, as it were, on Mount Sinai, and loudly proclaimed eternal perdition to a sinful world. Awful and extremely terrific was his message; nothing but the consuming flashes and dreadful thunders of the law, with hardly anything like the joyful sound of the Gospel. Endless condemnation, deserved by sinners, was what he set forth with unusual power and energy. His own spirit seemed to have been filled with great and awful terror. He appeared as if he wished to kindle the fire of hell around the transgressors of God's law, that he might terrify them. He unfolded the indignation of heaven against sin with amazing clearness, earnestness and vigour.[11]

Here again are Bunyan's stern captains, marching through the sermons of Daniel Rowland as he preached what he felt in his own soul. Under such ministry the people to whom he preached awoke from their spiritual stupor, but only to alarm and despair. It was a wise older minister, Philip Pugh, who therefore drew Rowland aside and ministered the gospel to him first and then advised him to preach the same to the wounded people:

---

11. Quoted in Eifion Evans, *Daniel Rowland and the Great Evangelical Awakening in Wales* (Edinburgh: Banner of Truth, 1985), 39.

"Preach the Gospel to the people, dear Sir, and apply the Balm of Gilead, the blood of Christ, to their spiritual wounds, and show the necessity of faith in the crucified Saviour." "I am afraid," said Rowland, "that I have not that faith myself in its vigour and full exercise." "Preach on it," said Pugh, "till you feel it in that way; no doubt it will come. If you go on preaching the law in this manner, you will kill half the people in the country, for you thunder out the curses of the law, and preach in such a terrific manner, that no-one can stand before you."[12]

So Rowland, and others with him, learned to bring the right tools to bear at the right time, to become what his biographer calls "both Boanerges and Evangelius, the complete Gospel preacher."[13] And as it must be in the broad strokes, so it must be in the personal dealings. We must be able to reach into the quiver of Scripture and pull forth the arrow suited to the particular target, to minister wisely and sensitively to the needy soul, whether to stir up or to bind up. Did not the apostle Paul himself know this?

> Knowing, therefore, the terror of the Lord, we persuade men; but we are well known to God, and I also trust are well known in your consciences. For we do not commend ourselves again to you, but give you opportunity to boast on our behalf, that you may have an answer for those who boast in appearance and not in heart. For if we are beside ourselves, it is for God; or if we are of sound mind, it is for you. For the love of Christ compels us, because we judge thus: that if One died for all, then all died; and He died for all, that those who live should live no longer for themselves, but for Him who died for them and rose again. Therefore, from now on, we regard no one according to the flesh. Even though we have known Christ according to the flesh, yet now we know Him thus no longer. Therefore, if anyone is in Christ, he is a new creation; old things have passed away; behold, all things have become new. Now all things are of God, who has reconciled us to Himself through Jesus Christ, and has given us the ministry

---

12. Evans, *Daniel Rowland*, 43.
13. Evans, *Daniel Rowland*, 45.

of reconciliation, that is, that God was in Christ reconciling the world to Himself, not imputing their trespasses to them, and has committed to us the word of reconciliation. Now then, we are ambassadors for Christ, as though God were pleading through us: we implore you on Christ's behalf, be reconciled to God. For He made Him who knew no sin to be sin for us, that we might become the righteousness of God in Him (2 Cor. 5:11–21).

When our quiver is well stocked, let us *fire our gospel arrows often and accurately*, being prepared both to learn to do better and to persevere in our activity. In archery, we have only a set number of shots. Sometimes in the discipline of evangelism, God in His mercy grants us a multitude of opportunities. We need to fire over and over with a variety of arrows. If the arrow of judgment fails, send down the barb of conscience. If the silver shaft of mercy will not work, send down the iron bolt of justice. Send what seems fit, as God directs. We might need to select and release many arrows over many hours before the bull's-eye is well struck. Who knows how often we must fire, perhaps even the same arrows, before we strike home? The first shot is sometimes the hardest:

> It is the first step that really costs effort. If a beginning is made, all is gained. If only, by the Spirit given in answer to that prayer of faith, you get over the shyness, the awkwardness, of a first trial or two,—if only you break the ice, and force yourself to let your lips be unsealed,—you will soon find that there really are no such formidable difficulties in that way as you were apt to anticipate; that it is not so hard a task after all to show forth God's praise.[14]

But it is not always the first shot that hits the mark. We hear of Hudson Taylor, founder of the China Inland Mission, who was ministering to a sick man of gross character. Visiting this man regularly to care for his body, Taylor would seek to speak each time of his soul's need. The man would each time turn his face away, and the young man would leave. Finally, Taylor felt that the effort was being wasted, and—for the first time—he stood to leave without speaking the truth concerning sin and salvation. The man called him back and asked whether he had

---

14. Candlish, *Prayer of a Broken Heart*, 79.

a word for his soul this time, and with sudden tears Taylor declared to him the love of Christ, and it proved the occasion of the hardhearted and stubborn man's conversion. So start shooting and keep shooting, for who knows what is hitting home and when the arrows will finally pierce to a person's soul.

Finally and vitally, let us *fletch our arrows with prayer*. As feathers are the means of arrows flying straight and true and far, so our gospel arrows must be fletched with prayer that they might find their target. The only thing that will bear gospel truth to the mark of a sinner's soul, so that we might make our mark, is the Spirit of God. Therefore we must pray. Without prayer our arrows will fall short and go awry. If that should happen, we accomplish nothing. Who makes a person a Christian? It is the Spirit of God. Every gospel arrow must be let fly with at least a whisper of prayer, that the Spirit of God would bear it to its target.

So far we have considered at some length the felt responsibility of the brokenhearted evangelist, but let us never fail to acknowledge that—whoever plants and waters—it is God who gives the increase (1 Cor. 3:6). We must reckon with the armor of spiritual deadness that is worn by sinners, an armor that is impervious to all but those arrows that are carried by divine power and directed by divine wisdom. So Paul declares, "The natural man does not receive the things of the Spirit of God, for they are foolishness to him; nor can he know them, because they are spiritually discerned" (1 Cor. 2:14). Unless the Spirit of God works with and by the Word of God, men and women will remain utterly unmoved.

Do you pray for those to whom you speak? For those who visit your church? Have you sought God's mercy to soften the hearts of those with whom you deal? When you deliver tracts or invitations, is there no time to send them with prayer, that God would bless them, that someone would take, read, and be saved? Do you pray that your arrows would be effectual? The Holy Spirit makes a person a Christian, and therefore it is to Him that we must cry in order that we might see sinners saved.

CHAPTER 5

AM I FRUITFUL?
Our Great Expectation

Let me begin this chapter with a challenge. You might have read this far quickly or slowly, but now I ask you this: How much of a difference have these questions about our willingness, effectiveness, commitment, and focus made to you so far? Have they altered the way in which you have thought about things or gone about them since you started reading? Perhaps you have read this in one sitting or have not yet had opportunities to put it all into practice, but, even so, have these things had an effect upon your mind and heart? Is it making a practical difference, prompting you to individual prayer and action, so that, rather than simply drifting along on the current of any corporate, church labors, you are wrapped up in a genuine and personal engagement in Christ's cause?

Will it keep making a difference? Will you be stirred up for a few moments, days, or months, and then slip back into indifference and inactivity? After a particular effort, we often flop back into a seat, thinking, "Phew, I'm glad that's over!" But this is to be an ongoing labor.

The Outcome of Our Evangelism

Look back over the last few days, weeks, or months of your life as a witness to Christ and at the activity of the church to which you belong. Consider that period in the light of the words that you have read here. What has been the impact of your witness to Christ on your family, friends, neighbors, and wider community? I trust that you will find much cause for rejoicing and encouragement as God answers your prayers. The glorious gospel of our Lord and Savior Jesus Christ is being proclaimed, and men and women who would never have known the gospel unless God in His sovereign grace had sent you to them have heard the Word of God preached and taught. The church, individually and corporately, and despite its many sins, shortcomings, frailties, and weaknesses, shows a desire and willingness to witness for her God and King. We are stirred to pursue the employment of our indispensable equipment; we use the means appointed by God with good conscience and a lively faith, preaching the truth by every legitimate means we can discern, pressing it home upon the consciences of those with whom we come into contact. We aim at genuine conversion, at true salvation—not merely the numerical increase of a congregation gathering in a building somewhere, not seeing unbelievers merely affected or improved, but sinners translated out of darkness into the kingdom of heaven and joining the people of God on their journey to the celestial city.

Do we see something of God's blessing upon those labors? I trust we do. Have you seen friends, colleagues, neighbors, family members, or people who were strangers to you until a few weeks past coming under the sound of the gospel, and perhaps coming back to hear more? Can you say with honesty that those who hear the gospel are genuinely affected by it and struck by the way you live it out as a Christian and as part of a church, so that even if some kick against the truth, no one can deny that faith in Christ makes a difference in the way you live? As you have engaged in the noble task of testimony, have you found your mind expanded, your heart quickened, your hand strengthened, and your prayers edged with fervor that previously they lacked?

I trust it is so and you are legitimately encouraged. But, brothers and sisters, calculate the outcome of your labors in absolute terms for a moment: What of *souls*? We must ask the question, "Am I fruitful?" Think not just of days or weeks; consider months or years. How many souls have professed faith under the preaching of the gospel in the church of which you are a member in the last twelve months or five years? How many men, women, boys, and girls do you have good grounds for supposing have actually been converted? For how many new spiritual lives has your church proved to be God's womb? In the salvation of how many sinners has our God granted you the humbling privilege of playing a part, however insignificant that part might appear?

Have you seen any open and consistent professions of faith in Jesus Christ, with those who make them being added to the church? If you have, have you seen many? Have you seen perhaps one or two, but not twenty? Have you seen twenty, but not fifty? Although there are times and places of blessing, and in these we rejoice, for many of us the sad reality is that we do not see the outcome of our evangelism producing, at the present time, a healthy crop of souls for Christ. We do not deny that a silent, private work may be still going on in the minds and hearts of some, but we may see no or few open professions of faith in Jesus Christ and few additions to the church of our Lord and Savior. Our gospel seed seems not to be falling on good ground. While there may be encouragements and blessings as we pursue the work and answers to our prayers, in absolute terms of seeing many (or perhaps even any) souls saved from sin, death, and hell, we have yet to see our aim achieved. We are still missing the mark.

Our Reaction to This Outcome
How should we deal with the often painful reality that fewer souls are regenerated in connection with our labors than we pray and hope for?

Can We Be Satisfied?
How can we be satisfied? How can we imagine that our task has been accomplished? I say it not to imply that you are sitting on your hands, but because there is a danger that you might end up doing so. How easy it is—especially if we have begun to make new efforts—simply to keep going at the pace and with the intensity of the present level. However, our aim and focus is conversion, and anything short of that, however creditable in its own terms, ought to grieve and disappoint us.

We cannot be satisfied with little fruit because there is simply too much at stake. This is not a discipline in which failure (in absolute terms), however honorable, can bring us joy. Our efforts, if they are not ultimately successful, make us not the aroma of life unto life, but rather the aroma of death unto death for those who are perishing (2 Cor. 2:16). Preaching and teaching and witnessing are never neutral activities; they either draw people to Christ or heighten their present condemnation.

Can we be satisfied simply with laying a weight of judgment upon the heads of those we love and for whom we care? Can we be satisfied that, with all our imperfections and sins and weaknesses, we have sincerely sought to placard Christ as crucified and risen before men, women, and children, and yet none or painfully few have bowed the knee to our Lord and King? Every knee will one day bow to Him, and every tongue will confess that He is Lord, to the glory of God the Father, but how few have done so now and might only do so in the terror of the Day of Judgment? Can we be content with our God and Lord—the Christ who loved us and gave Himself for us—being rejected by the ungodly? Can we be satisfied that some of our dear family members, friends, and neighbors have heard the truths concerning eternity for weeks, months, and perhaps years, and seem, rather than turning to Christ, to have become increasingly hardened to the all-too-familiar pleas of preachers, parents, and friends to come to Christ, to taste and see that the Lord is good? We see those whom we love sitting under the sound of gospel preaching as if it meant nothing and walking away apparently untouched by what they hear. Can we be satisfied when those for whose salvation we yearn seem to respond with such lack of feeling and desire? Can we be satisfied to know even that some few have come, but there are those still utterly caught up in the deceptive miseries of ungodliness? Are we not longing to see Christ glorified as countless ransomed slaves come into His kingdom, exalting Him as the redeemer who delivers from death? Are we satisfied with only one of our children saved? Are we content with a proportion of the congregation regenerate? Can we sleep easy with a few spiritual gains while a world passes by outside that cares nothing for the things of God? Thankful for what we have, we yet desire more.

Charles C. Luther was a New England minister who heard a preacher named A. H. Upham tell the story of a young man who, a month after being saved, was injured in an accident. It soon became clear that the injury was fatal. A Christian at the young man's bedside asked if he were afraid to die. The young man replied, "Friend, no, I am not afraid to die; for Jesus has saved me. But I have not been able to lead even one, such as I was, to Christ in the time I have known him. No, I am not afraid to die; but oh, if I go, must I go and empty-handed?" Profoundly moved, Luther began to write, and produced the following hymn:

"Must I go, and empty-handed,"
Thus my dear Redeemer meet?
Not one day of service give Him,
Lay no trophy at His feet?

"Must I go, and empty-handed?"
Must I meet my Savior so?
Not one soul with which to greet Him,
Must I empty-handed go?

Not at death I shrink or falter,
For my Savior saves me now;
But to meet Him empty-handed,
Thought of that now clouds my brow.

Oh, the years in sinning wasted,
Could I but recall them now,
I would give them to my Savior,
To His will I'd gladly bow.

Oh, ye saints, arouse, be earnest,
Up and work while yet 'tis day;
Ere the night of death o'ertake thee,
Strive for souls while still you may.

How fearful to imagine that an unbeliever can be satisfied with his lot, and yet it is true. Family members, friends, neighbors, and colleagues seem content to be on the way to hell, not knowing whether the next step might carry them to that fearful destination for all eternity. They rest easy as the light shines while they still sit in darkness. They are often blissfully unaware that they are dead in trespasses and sins, and all the while everlasting life is held out in Christ Jesus. Some rest on the fringes of life, a vague hope or desire to have life, without knowing for sure that they are Christ's and He is theirs. And we are the ones who can call on them to consider their ways and be wise. We can, under God, turn them from godlessness and to Christ for salvation. Can we be satisfied with anything less?

Should We Be Distressed?

Brothers and sisters, how could we be anything but distressed? Christ is perhaps preached in our midst, but not honored by believing faith in those who have heard. Those whom we love still labor under sentence of condemnation. Some to whom we speak seem closer to the kingdom, but how many seem to be more in darkness now than they have ever been? Not only that, but we are conscious of so many sins and failings in our own efforts to proclaim Christ that may be to some degree responsible for the fact that we have not persuaded anyone to trust in Christ. We are sadly confident that—should God look to us for a reason not to bless our efforts—one moment's scrutiny under the divine gaze would reveal a thousand reasons we do not deserve to see any fruit from our labors.

What is our response to these things? Does our lack of fruitfulness in the pursuit of souls make us shrug, or does it make us weep? If we can only shrug, we ought to be thoroughly ashamed and repent with tears over a most criminal hardness of heart. Our Savior wept over Jerusalem. This was His city, the one to which He had sent the prophets, desiring that He might gather its citizens as a hen gathers its chicks under her wings, but Jerusalem was not willing. She stoned those who were sent to her, and, toward the end of His life, when our Savior came up on the road again and saw Jerusalem, He wept. Tears poured from His eyes at the prospect of the condemnation of the city that had seen so many blessings of gospel truth proclaimed in it, and yet had not believed (Luke 13:34–35; 19:41–42). If Christ cried out and wept over Jerusalem, can we not cry out and weep over our families, friends, streets, neighborhoods, towns, and cities? If when Paul, Christ's bondservant, took his leave of the Ephesian elders, he could testify that he had not ceased to warn everyone night and day with tears (Acts 20:31), can we be content to shrug our shoulders at the great need of the godless to turn from their sins and idols and to serve the living and true God and to wait for His Son from heaven? Christ and those closest to Him in spirit and character are grieved when the gospel is preached and sinners are not saved.

We ought to be distressed that sinners hear the truth and are not converted. We feel something of the distress they ought to feel. We ought to be distressed when people have come close and turned away. We ought to be distressed when life has been held out, but is not yet possessed. We ought to be grieved in our souls because Christ has been present, and some have not bowed the knee to Him. All the opportunity needed has already been given to some—that they would have no complaint if Christ were to snatch them away this moment to judgment—but the day is far past, and they are not saved. How can we be anything but distressed that salvation is at hand, but not in the hands of those for whose life we long! They still hang condemned over the gulf of an eternity under God's just punishment for sins, and are we able to contemplate such an end without at least some spark of concern in our souls? If Christ wept over sinners, should we not weep over them when they will not weep for themselves?

Should We Be Downcast?

Despite all our legitimate sorrow at present unfruitfulness, Psalm 51:13 tells us that we ought not to be downcast: "Then I will teach transgressors Your ways, and sinners shall be converted to You." Satisfied we cannot be, distressed we certainly ought to be, but downcast we can never be, for we anticipate that as we shoot our gospel arrows with prayer, faith, diligence, and persistence at the heart of transgressors, sinners shall be converted to God. We have a great expectation. We are entitled to expect that, as we teach transgressors God's ways, sinners will be turned back to God. John Calvin says that "we are too apt to conclude that our attempts at reclaiming the ungodly are vain and ineffectual, and forget that God is able to crown them with success."[1] While we may not immediately see the fruit we desire and cannot be satisfied with such an outcome, and while we can only grieve and mourn over so much hardness and so little brokenness of heart around us, we should not be cast down. It was never up to us in the first place. We have been given the means and the promise. We may seem to have been ineffectual in reclaiming the ungodly, but let us not forget that God is able to crown even our efforts with success.

---

1. John Calvin, *Commentaries* (Grand Rapids: Baker, 1996), 5:302.

Here is hope too for the unbeliever: there is a gospel being proclaimed which is the power of God to salvation for everyone who
believes. Anyone still outside, looking in at the rich feast spread for
God's children, may come to the door of salvation and, bowing the
knee, enter in, for no one is excluded who comes with repentance, trusting in Jesus to deliver him from the judgment of sin.

Our Abiding Conviction

I want now to concentrate on one thing from Psalm 51:13: it is God's
sovereign pleasure and solemn promise to crown faithful gospel preaching with genuine gospel success. "I will teach transgressors Your ways,
and *sinners shall be converted to You*." Can you see it plainly there in the
text, the connection between teaching transgressors God's ways and
the salvation of sinners? When we do the one, the other will follow,
just as night follows day and day follows night. The faithful declaration of God's truth to the ungodly will result in sinners seeking their
God in repentance and faith. Do you believe that? Do you believe, even
weeping over unbelief on every hand, that the faithful instruction of
transgressors in God's gracious ways by men and women who know
the joy of salvation and the realities of Spirit-sealed living will have as
its consequence the return of sinners to God? Do you believe that for
yourself, in your own witness to Christ? Do you believe that for the
church of which Christ has made you a part? Before we get swept up so
high that our feet are no longer planted upon the ground of reality, let
us also affirm certain caveats.

When?

We cannot say when this will occur. It might be many years in the future
that fruit might be borne of our present efforts, long after some of us who
labor and pray have ourselves gone to be with our Lord (if Christ does
not first return). Who knows how many words of truth will come back
to the minds of those who have read them? Who knows if some of those
who hear preaching outside church buildings might travel thousands of
miles before remembering that they once heard someone offer salvation
from sins in Christ Jesus and repent and believe for their salvation? A

young boy named Luke Short once heard the eminent Puritan John Flavel preaching in Dartmouth. That boy grew and immigrated to New England, leading a life without much thought of God. Michael Boland describes what happened years later: "One day as [Luke Short] sat in his fields reflecting upon his long life, he recalled a sermon he had heard in Dartmouth as a boy before he sailed to America. The horror of dying under the curse of God was impressed upon him as he meditated on the words he had heard so long ago and he was converted to Christ— eighty-five years after hearing John Flavel preach."[2]

The words Short heard so many years before from the faithful preacher of God's Word came back to his mind with converting power, and he was saved through the instrumentality of a decades-old sermon. Perhaps parents whose children now are heading away from God will one day welcome their once-wayward offspring into the land of glory. Perhaps some of those nameless and faceless strangers for whom we pray shall, as a result of our prayers, be brought to faith in Christ many years after our praying tongues have been silenced by death. It might be immediate: Why should we not expect people to come in, hear, and be saved? Is that not within God's power? It is not impossible that a sinner of any stripe should walk through the doors of a church building during a sermon or overhear two Christians speaking of their beloved Savior[3] or pick up a tract or return to an old invitation or bump into an old friend recently converted, and be within moments redeemed from sin and death and hell. God's power is sufficient to prevent us imposing any limitations of time, either of shortness or length. We cannot say when sinners will be converted.

How Many?

We cannot say how many will be saved because we know that many are called, but few are chosen. We might long to see multitudes pressing

---

2. Michael Boland, publisher's introduction to *The Mystery of Providence*, by John Flavel (Edinburgh: Banner of Truth, 1963), 11.

3. John Bunyan's experience, recorded in *Grace Abounding to the Chief of Sinners* (p. 14), was of overhearing "three or four poor women" speaking about spiritual realities in such a way as completely to expose his own self-righteousness.

into the kingdom from the darkest ends of the earth, having heard and believed the gospel. Some may see sinners crowding into the kingdom. Others see one here, two there, five or ten over a few years, as the God of heaven and earth is pleased by various and gracious means to draw His elect to His Son, the Lord Jesus. We should not despise small advances, though we might long for days of great blessing. We know that some do reject the gospel, and that makes us realists as we preach and teach, but biblical realism also says that when the gospel is preached and sinners are taught God's ways, some shall be converted to Him. We do not need to know how many, but we can be assured that some will hear and believe.

Who?

We cannot say who will be saved, for that lies hidden in the secret and eternal counsels of God. This verse does not open up for us the pages of the Book of Life in which the names of the chosen are recorded. Nobody knows that book but God Himself. If we spend our lives trying to figure out whether our own names are in this book, we will likely spend our lives either without believing or lacking assurance of our salvation, because that book is largely closed to us. Our job is not to discover whether someone is elect or even to discern our own election ahead of believing. We are called upon to believe in order that we might have life everlasting. Faith proves election; it does not tremble about it. We simply do not know who will be saved. Election is none of our business, in that sense: we know it, believe it, and preach it—even rely upon it. We do not consider our hands tied by it but rather our tongues liberated to declare the gospel to every creature in the sure knowledge that Christ will have His own and that our testimony will be the means He employs to call them. It is not for us to pick or predict and preach only on that basis, but freely to proclaim the gospel abroad and trust that by His appointed means God will gather in all upon whom He has set His love.

How?

We cannot say how God will convert sinners, whether it will be under the public preaching of the Word, as we would definitely expect, or through hearing a tape or CD, watching a video or DVD, reading a tract or booklet, listening to sermons or other material streamed online, through flicking disinterestedly through some massive tome of profound learning or some simple treatment of basic truth, or through the earnest words of a husband or wife, son or daughter, father or mother, friend or stranger. We cannot say whether it will be public or private or the particular scriptural mode of dealing that God might use in any individual case. Where does the wind come from? Where does it go? We do not know where it comes from or where it goes, but we can tell when it is passing or has passed. So it is with the Spirit of God. We cannot assure ourselves or anyone else of precisely how God will use His truth in redemption, how He will reveal Christ to some benighted soul.

How Long?

We cannot say how long we must preach and teach and pray before we see such an outcome. We are entitled to hope that it might be seconds, but it can be days or years. For some, faith follows hearing within moments, as the gospel flashes like lightning upon their conscience; for others, it follows slowly and gradually, as the dawning of the day, with the darkness of spiritual night slowly chased away by the rays of the rising Sun of Righteousness. Many years of gospel instruction and earnest prayer might be required with some before the appointed day of their salvation arrives. God does not say, "When you teach transgressors My ways, if they don't get it within a month, they're out!" He says, "Sinners shall be converted" but there is no guarantee or promise as to how long that will take.

What Truth?

We cannot say what truth God will be pleased to use to bring any particular sinner to Himself. David says it is by teaching "God's ways," and while the great realities of the gospel must surely be preeminent, that is a broad and beautiful spectrum of doctrine. It might be God's electing love, some specific aspect of the person of Christ, the pouring out of the Spirit of God, the Old Testament requirements for worship, the condemnation of the wicked, the heavenly joys of the saints. Turn to any page in your Bible: God never declared that He would never use those particular truths to save sinners. It might be those that we esteem most likely to be profitable; it could be those that we imagine most unlikely, or even improbable. Consider the sheer range of Scripture, and imagine the list of texts that have been preached on to the saving of a soul, the topics that have been God's means of bringing trouble to the careless and peace to the troubled.[4] Such a list takes us from Genesis to Revelation; roams topically from Dan to Beersheba; encompasses some of the more abstruse doctrines; deals with people, places, and particular teachings; and runs the gamut of truth. And yet, as the scope and substance of the Bible is exposed in all its parts, as transgressors are taught God's ways, sinners down through the centuries have been converted to God.

But let us not be foolish and set out to test God by seeking the most difficult and least applicable portions to teach and hoping for a blessing. That is to run against sense. If you want to catch fish, let down the net. There are particular portions of God's Word that seem almost designed to bring people from darkness to light, and the most plainly glorious and winning of God's ways are those He makes known in salvation by His Son. Again, Spurgeon speaks as a soul winner:

> I believe that *those sermons which are fullest of Christ are the most likely to be blessed to the conversion of the hearers*. Let your sermons be full of Christ, from beginning to end crammed full of the gospel. As for myself, brethren, I cannot preach anything else but Christ and His cross, for I know nothing else, and long ago, like the apostle Paul, I determined not to know anything else save Jesus Christ and Him crucified. People have often asked me, "What is the secret of your success?" I always answer that I have no other secret but this, that I have preached the gospel,—not about the gospel, but the gospel,—the full, free, glorious gospel of the living Christ who is the incarnation of the good news. Preach Jesus Christ, brethren, always and everywhere; and every time you preach be sure to have much of Jesus Christ in the sermon.

---

4. Consider Jonathan Edwards, "A Narrative of Surprising Conversions," in *Jonathan Edwards on Revival* (Edinburgh: Banner of Truth, 1965), 44–74, for a demonstration of such variety in experience.

You remember the story of the old minister who heard a sermon by a young man, and when he was asked by the preacher what he thought of it he was rather slow to answer, but at last he said, "If I must tell you, I did not like it at all; there was no Christ in your sermon." "No," answered the young man, "because I did not see that Christ was in the text." "Oh!" said the old minister, "but do you not know that from every little town and village and tiny hamlet in England there is a road leading to London? Whenever I get hold of a text, I say to myself, 'There is a road from here to Jesus Christ, and I mean to keep on His track till I get to Him.'" "Well," said the young man, "but suppose you are preaching from a text that says nothing about Christ?" "Then I will go over hedge and ditch but what I will get at Him." So must we do, brethren; we must have Christ in all our discourses, whatever else is in or not in them. There ought to be enough of the gospel in every sermon to save a soul. Take care that it is so when you are called to preach before Her Majesty the Queen, and if you have to preach to chairwomen or chairmen, still always take care that there is the real gospel in every sermon.[5]

Given the opportunity, and with the aim of saving sinners uppermost, those portions that make Christ most plain, depict Him as most excellent, reveal Him as perfectly suited to the needs of sinners, those texts that direct to or demand a Savior, are to be relied upon and heavily employed. At the same time, sermons and conversations and comments that you might think are completely outlandish or dry might be the means of God saving one or another wretched sinner, bringing truth to bear by His Spirit upon the mind and heart of an unconverted human being, as a result of which a sinner is converted to God. Let us not be so soon convinced that God cannot use this preacher or that topic or this series or that church or this conversation for the salvation of His elect. When did it ever lie with man to save? Again, this is not to say that we avoid those glorious central truths of Christ and Him crucified or that we do not preach Christ from all the Scriptures. However, we are

5. Charles H. Spurgeon, *The Soul Winner* (Grand Rapids: Eerdmans, 1994), 106–7.

confident that God is able to use more than a "Calvary sermon" to give rest to a burdened heart. Show us a truehearted servant of God prayerfully pouring out his energies in the declaration of God's truth, making Christ known in all the Bible, and we will show you a man whom we are confident the Spirit might use at any moment to usher a soul into Christ's kingdom.

There are a thousand things that we cannot begin to guess and are not for us to know. However, we do know this: the undertaking God here promises to crown with genuine gospel success is the persistent, accurate, prayerful, earnest, diligent, consistent, principled teaching of His ways to transgressors.

> For as the rain comes down, and the snow from heaven,
> And do not return there,
> But water the earth,
> And make it bring forth and bud,
> That it might give seed to the sower
> And bread to the eater,
> So shall My word be that goes forth from My mouth;
> It shall not return to Me void,
> But it shall accomplish what I please,
> And it shall prosper in the thing for which I sent it (Isa. 55:10–11).

Bowing to God's sovereign right and pleasure to bless His Word by His Spirit—when, to how many, to whom, how, and after how long He chooses—so as to glorify His name and accomplish all His glorious purposes of wisdom and grace, our conviction remains that God will bless the faithful proclamation of gospel truth with conversions.

Our Response to This Conviction

If this is our conviction and these are our concerns and hopes, then how do we respond to these things? What are the lessons that we must learn?

A Criticism

Let conscience point its finger at your heart. Ask yourself with Judgment Day honesty, "Am I doing my part? Am I engaging in this task with all that I have and am? Do I pray as I should? Am I present in my appointed place when God's Word is preached? Do I deliver spoken or written invitations to Christ, or at least to hear Christ preached, earnestly, graciously, warmly, and persistently? Do I plead, preach, entreat, as I could and should? Am I as earnest as I ought to be? Am I as clear as I could be? Do I take my opportunities to warn, exhort, invite, and encourage unbelievers in my circle to turn to Christ for salvation? Do I point people to Christ? Do I plead, even with tears, that the members of my own family might look to Christ and be saved? Do I press home on my unsaved children the saving truth of God's Word? Do I labor in the church where God has put me, in concert with my brothers and sisters in Christ and on my own initiative? Do I enter into these works with the right motives and desires for the honor and glory of God and out of a love for the souls of men and women?"

Let us not hide behind the sovereignty of God at this point, becoming crippled by a practical hyper-Calvinism disguised behind an orthodox declaration of a God to whom salvation belongs. When the wedding feast was ready and those who had been first invited were careless and neglectful, then the master said to the servant, "Go out into the highways and hedges, and compel them to come in, that my house may be filled" (Luke 14:23). He calls upon those sent to bring the invitation to bear forcefully and urgently with a view to seeing the house filled with those who heed. It is because God is sovereign that we go out and press home the claims of truth upon the consciences of people.

But is your conscience clear with regard to these things? Has every reader of these pages done all that he or she might have done? If not, beloved friends, and if our conscience accuses us, then let us cry out in repentance to God for the covering of our sins and for grace to fall so far short no longer, but to pursue the path of righteousness with faith and vigor.

A Comfort

We are entitled, on the basis of God's own Word, to a righteous and legitimate expectation of success. That success does not depend ultimately upon our strength or gifts. We are to employ them, yes, and God has promised to bless the diligent use of them, and that is where human responsibility must be wedded to divine sovereignty. This, though, is a matter of faith, not of pride, ignorance, or stupidity. It has already been true and will continue to be true. Can you begin to estimate the number of men and women who have been converted through reading or hearing preached the words of Psalm 51 in the years since David first penned it? How many have found healing for a broken heart here? How many powerful sermons have been preached from these beautiful and lucid words that have been the means, in the Spirit's hands, of bringing sinners to Christ? In these verses, David is teaching transgressors God's ways, and sinners have been converted to God. We are entitled to an expectation of success. We can go on laboring with this great expectation, trusting and praying that God would bless us more exceedingly abundantly than ever we could ask or think. Have our efforts so far appeared to be vain and ineffectual? Let us go on using God's appointed means, because He is well able to crown our endeavors with success. We are to look to the Almighty for a blessing: sowing and watering as men, it will always be God who brings forth fruit. Are we not entitled to pray to God to prove Himself gloriously true to His Word? Are we not entitled to ask for many souls, and soon? Can we not ask God to pour out His blessing upon the preaching? Are we going beyond God's Word in asking Him to send His Spirit down in our midst so that every unconverted person hearing the gospel preached among us should look to Jesus Christ and be saved? Can we not plead that the teaching of our own children, the instruction of our own friends and neighbors, might be crowned with gospel success? We can pray this promise back to God, and with confidence, looking to the hand of our God until He has mercy upon us, earnestly pleading for fruit from the seed that has been sown. We are entitled to expect God to bless His own Word.

A Challenge

This challenges us in the realm of *commitment*. What should we do in the light of an apparent immediate lack of fruit, of apparent limited gospel success? Do we change the means, alter the message, and downgrade the aim? Perhaps the music is a little old-fashioned and the psalms and hymns are a bit long and complicated? Maybe the Scripture readings could be reduced? Could the sermons be cut back to about fifteen minutes at a time? Maybe if we had a band, if we had someone younger, if we got a "celebrity" to speak, if we dressed more trendily, if we moved the seats, if we used our lighting better…. We could imagine a thousand possibilities of changing the means, the method, the aim, and even of rearranging the furniture. Perhaps we should just concentrate on attracting people into our church buildings first, and then we can figure out how to teach them later? Maybe we should just try to gather a crowd and grow the congregation? Should we avoid driving after people's consciences and just step back and chat or "share," rather than proclaim a Christ who is to be believed upon by all in order that they might be saved? Do we introduce the carnality of the world into our worship of God with the aim of making it more attractive, not to the God of our salvation but to the godless wanderer? Do we seek a different, more palatable gospel and begin to shave and pare away the rough edges of redeeming truth? Do we concentrate on growing our congregation numerically and molding them into a more respectable group of men and women before we go after their souls as tokens of grace? God forbid! Neither do we need regress into the past, as if merely being old-fashioned—sometimes several centuries out of date—guaranteed success or demonstrated unusual holiness. Some sincere believers seem to take a perverse delight in making the saving truth as inaccessible and remote as possible, hidden behind a thousand unnecessary walls of obscurity and seeming irrelevance, as if to mummify the gospel, embalming it in the dusty wrappings of ages past, masking its immediate vitality in the unnecessary trappings of centuries long gone.

The issue is not relative antiquity and novelty. There is filth and froth and folly in every age, and against it all the truth of God stands. This is the issue: What is true, and how can I honor God in the declaration of it? Our language, our dress, our worship, our friendship, our accessibility must never be a mere aping of the world or a respectfully dry duplication of long-dead saints, but must uphold the honor of God and the spiritual distinctiveness of His redeemed people even while we communicate that God saves sinners of all kinds here and now.

We must then be committed to the plain, earnest, biblical proclamation of the ways of God to transgressors. We stand in the old paths,
declare the truths that God has committed to us, plowing and sowing and trusting in God to give the increase. The temptation is to leave
those paths, but we are called upon to proclaim God's truth in God's
manner and to rely upon God to give the blessing.

Can we improve? God willing, we can, because we are not as good
at employing those God-appointed means as we ought to be. We can set
out to do what God commands us to do in a way that is far purer and
higher and more God-honoring than before, but it is simply not part of
the possible range of responses to this situation either to depart from
or to exchange God's appointed means for anyone or anything else that
the world, the flesh, and the devil might suggest as the better way to
bring sinners into the kingdom. We are called upon to teach transgressors God's ways and, God helping us, we must revive our endeavors,
we must pour ourselves out yet more earnestly, but we must not rely
upon means that God has not appointed, still less employ those things
that are contrary to His appointment. Here we stand, and we cannot
and must not shift. Let us never cease to improve in our employment
of God's appointed means, but let us never dally with the prospect of
exchanging those means for any that God has not identified.

This challenges us in the sphere of *prayer*. Have we pleaded
with God more earnestly as a result of these things? Will you plead
this promise of Psalm 51:13, and plead it more vigorously than ever
before? Could it be our prayers that, under God, push some of these
lost ones over the edge into salvation? Have you seen what seem to be
the beginnings of God's grace at work in anyone or what might be the
glimmerings of faith in Christ? In Christ's parable of the sower who
went forth to sow in Matthew 13, three of the four soils on which the
seed fell gave a hint of potential fruitfulness. Admittedly, with some the
birds came in before the seed ever took root. But two of those that at
first seemed to promise fruit proved to be vain and empty; there were
some with whom the seed started to spring up, and it withered under
persecution or was choked by the cares of the world.

But when the seed starts to spring up, might it not be that these are the ones whom God is drawing to Himself, and will our prayers not follow them as we plead with God that He might bring these things to pass? Will you plead it in general terms, for the church of Christ in every place? Will you plead it specifically for those individuals whose eternal well-being the Lord God has laid upon your heart, those who are no longer nameless and faceless but who have been in our midst, and whom—if we are anything like Jesus Christ—we have begun to love and to yearn for their salvation? We have seen and spoken to them, and we know them to be human beings with immortal souls. If that does not stir us up to pray, "O God of grace, give me this man, give me this woman! May your Word be effectual in bringing and uniting this one to Jesus Christ! Grant that your Spirit might so work as to turn this one utterly and entirely from sin to faith in Jesus Christ! Lord, give us these people!" then nothing will. Are we pouring ourselves out in prayer and supplication before God, coming to private and public prayer with our minds and hearts fixed and stirred and well-stocked with the truth of God so that we can plead earnestly and effectively with the prayers of the righteous, that God would be pleased to make this true for us in these days? Will you plead this promise for the honor and glory of the Christ whom you adore and serve and for whose honor and glory you will, God helping, give all that you have and are to have more manifest in this fallen world?

It challenges us in the area of *activity*. We might at times feel ready to collapse in a heap for a while, but our rest will come with Christ in glory. Now is the time to be up and doing, without slackening or sinful laziness. If these are God's appointed means, then I should give myself to them, pour myself into them, allowing none to outstrip me in the pursuit of God's glory by them. Will you endeavor, God helping you, that no one will surpass you in your personal pursuit of the effective communication of gospel truth? Yes, we have different gifts, graces, callings, and opportunities, but we have one God and one business in our lives, and that is to glorify Him.

Putting aside all excuses about what we are or are not, imagine that you stood side by side with your identical twin. Would you undertake to enter into holy competition in order that, all other things being equal, he or she will not outdo you in the faithful, diligent, persistent, accurate, prayerful, earnest communication of gospel truth concerning Christ and Him crucified to needy sinners? Perhaps you need to begin with something simple and straightforward and in company with a friend for encouragement and courage. When we set out on a training regime or attempt something beyond our normal scope and regular sphere, giving up is easy, often before we have begun. But a running partner, a friend to urge us on and be urged on by us, a relationship of mutual encouragement, can be the difference between grand ideas coming to nothing and small seeds growing into great trees. Shall we, then, undertake to begin to begin to begin? Do we aim in due course to excel in the proclamation of Christ to sinners? Are we willing as churches to set out to bring sinners in? Spurgeon makes his plea this way:

> So, try to get at close quarters with sinners; talk gently to them till you have whispered them into the kingdom of heaven, till you have told into their ears the blessed story that will bring peace and joy to their heart. We want, in the Church of Christ, a band of well-trained sharpshooters, who will pick the people out individually, and be always on the watch for all who come into the place, not annoying them, but making sure that they do not go away without having had a personal warning, a personal invitation, and a personal exhortation to come to Christ. We want to train all our people for this service, so as to make Salvation Armies out of them. Every man, woman, or child who is in our churches should be set to work for the Lord.[6]

Spurgeon might have had in mind one of his elders at the Tabernacle. Those elders generally sat with the minister on the platform, and the great preacher was occasionally aware, during his closing prayer, that one of the elders had left his side. When he looked up he would find that man sliding onto a seat, near somebody whom he had identified during the course of the preaching as being unusually affected under the sound of the gospel. That dear man was one of Spurgeon's

6. Spurgeon, *Soul Winner*, 135.

snipers, and he would go after those who were within sight of the kingdom and press them home. When you have visitors in the church, do you speak with them only about their jobs, families, and the hotness or coldness or dryness or wetness of the weather? How many have you been inviting, exhorting, and pressing into the kingdom of heaven?

On any given Lord's Day in our churches, there might be several who desire some lengthy conversation with the pastors, and there are people who are unconverted who are passing by. But how many of us are picking up those to whom the elders cannot speak? How many of us are sharpshooters in the army of Jesus Christ? Do you see someone bowed at the end of the sermon? Are you the one who goes alongside and asks, "Friend, is there something weighing down your soul? Can I help?" Do you see someone stand, ready to walk away from or make light of the sermon? Are you the one who, rather than going to sweep that person along on the tide of unsanctified conversation, says, "Rather than all that, what of those things you have just heard?" Are you the one who draws alongside the children or teenagers and, addressing them with all gentleness and tenderness, says to them that you desire their salvation, perhaps taking up the terms of the message just delivered? No one or two or three of us are sufficient for this work. All the church must be working, and we must undertake that no one else, according to their God-given capacity, will outstrip us in our faithful and loving endeavors to see sinners brought to Jesus Christ.

Finally, it challenges us with regard to our *faith*. Do you believe that God can do this? Do you believe that through the preaching of the gospel here, and through your individual efforts, God can save sinners? Have we allowed a false humility to persuade us that God would never use our efforts to save sinners while we are yet distressed that no one has so far been saved? Our fundamental problem may not be misplaced modesty, but lack of faith. It never is dependent on us; it will never be dependent on any of us. If we spend our days looking to self, we will have nothing to show for it except much bemoaning of our own shortcomings. Why should we imagine that God will bless us without any faithful expectation? Do we come into our church gatherings with expectant hope that, as sinners are taught the ways of God, they will be converted to Him? Do we come with a righteous, sustained, scriptural, holy expectation that as the gospel in Christ Jesus is proclaimed, sinners shall be saved? Anything else is unbelief. We should not look to ourselves, but to God and His promises. Again, as Calvin reminds us, "we are too apt to conclude that our attempts at reclaiming the ungodly are vain and ineffectual, and forget that God is able to crown them with success."[7] Let us cease looking to and depending on self and rather rest upon God in His power and His promises, and plead with Him—as we engage faithfully, prayerfully, earnestly, diligently, and consistently in the principled declaration of God's ways to those who need to be saved—that He would be pleased to turn sinners back to Himself. Let us cry out to God in confidence to crown our efforts with gospel success, and then set ourselves to the task in dependence upon our Christ, whose finished work is our hope, and the hope of all the world.

---

7. Calvin, *Commentaries*, 5:302.

SCRIPTURE INDEX